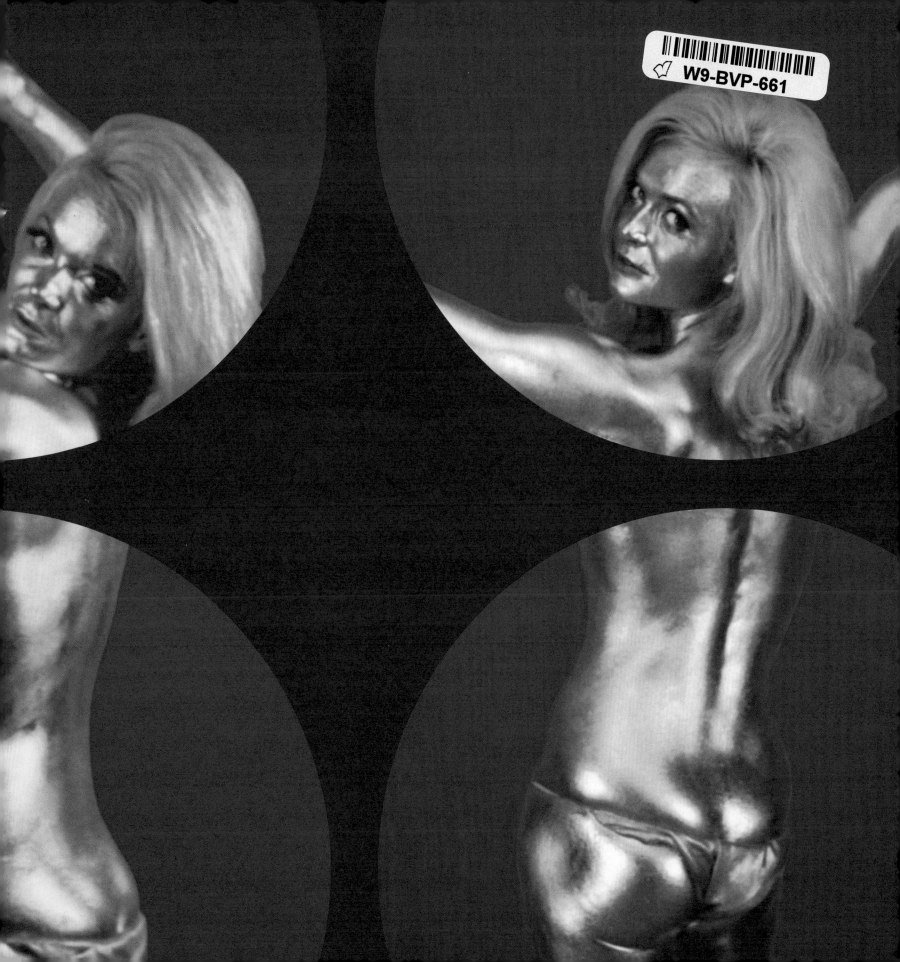

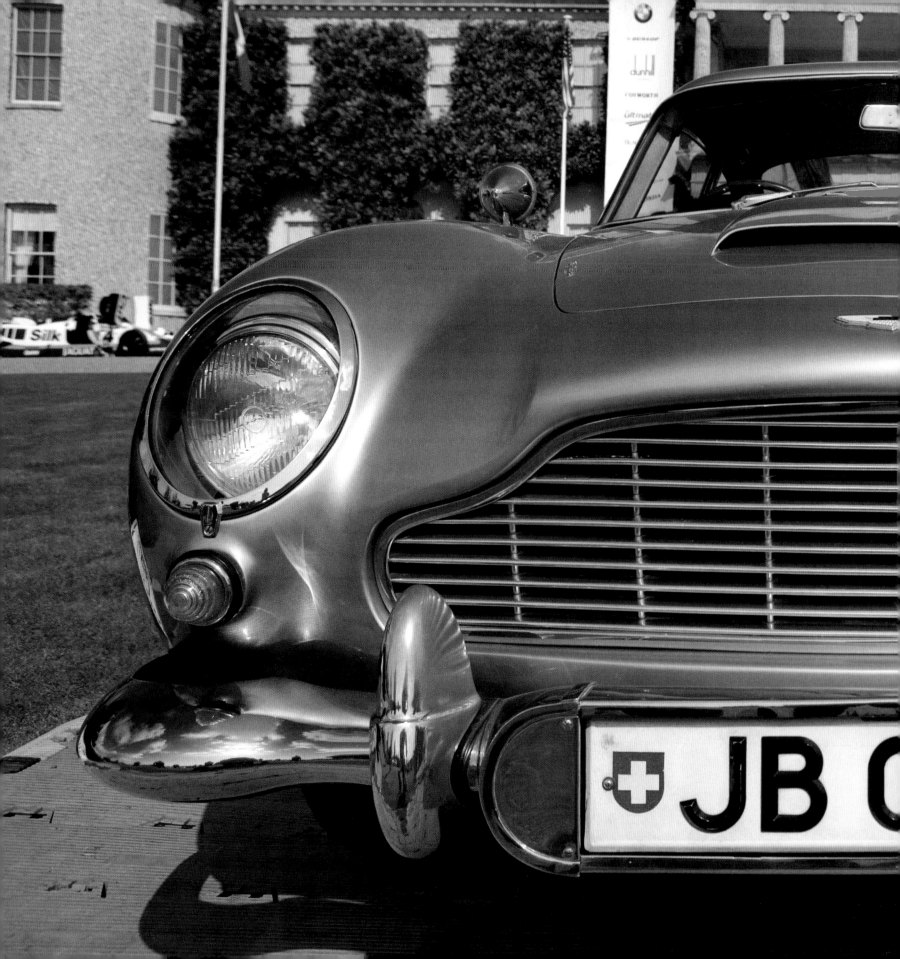

LIFE BOOKS

Managing Editor
Robert Sullivan

Director of Photography
Barbara Baker Burrows

Creative Director
Anke Stohlmann

Deputy Picture Editor
Christina Lieberman

Writer-Reporters
Michelle DuPré (Chief), Marilyn Fu

Copy Chief
Parlan McGaw

Copy Editors
Don Armstrong, Barbara Gogan

Photo Associate
Sarah Cates

Editorial Associate
Courtney Mifsud

Special Contributing Writers
Richard Corliss, Len Feldman

Consulting Picture Editors
Mimi Murphy (Rome), Tala Skari (Paris)

Editorial Director
Stephen Koepp

Editorial Operations Director
Michael Q. Bullerdick

EDITORIAL OPERATIONS

Richard K. Prue (Director), Brian
Fellows (Manager), Richard Shaffer
(Production), Keith Aurelio, Charlotte
Coco, Tracey Eure, Kevin Hart, Mert
Kerimoglu, Rosalie Khan, Patricia Koh,
Marco Lau, Brian Mai, Po Fung Ng, Rudi
Papiri, Robert Pizaro, Barry Pribula,
Clara Renauro, Katy Saunders, Hia Tan,
Vaune Trachtman

TIME HOME ENTERTAINMENT

Publisher Jim Childs

**Vice President, Business Development &
Strategy** Steven Sandonato

Executive Director, Marketing Services
Carol Pittard

Executive Director, Retail & Special Sales
Tom Mifsud

Executive Publishing Director
Joy Butts

Director, Bookazine Development & Marketing
Laura Adam

Finance Director Glenn Buonocore

Associate Publishing Director
Megan Pearlman

Assistant General Counsel
Helen Wan

Assistant Director, Special Sales
Ilene Schreider

Book Production Manager
Suzanne Janso

Design & Prepress Manager
Anne-Michelle Gallero

Brand Manager Roshni Patel

Associate Prepress Manager
Alex Voznesenskiy

Assistant Brand Manager
Stephanie Braga

Special thanks: Katherine Barnet,
Jeremy Biloon, Susan Chodakiewicz,
Rose Cirrincione, Lauren Hall Clark,
Jacqueline Fitzgerald, Christine Font,
Jenna Goldberg, Hillary Hirsch, David
Kahn, Amy Mangus, Robert Marasco,
Kimberly Marshall, Amy Migliaccio,
Nina Mistry, Dave Rozzelle, Ricardo
Santiago, Adriana Tierno, Vanessa Wu

ISBN 10: 1-61893-031-1
ISBN 13: 978-1-61893-031-6

Library of Congress Control Number:
2012933353

"LIFE" is a registered trademark of
Time Inc.

We welcome your comments and
suggestions about LIFE Books.
Please write to us at:
LIFE Books
Attention: Book Editors
PO Box 11016
Des Moines, IA 50336-1016

If you would like to order any of our
hardcover Collector's Edition books,
please call us at 1-800-327-6388
(Monday–Friday, 7 a.m.–8 p.m., or
Saturday, 7 a.m.–6 p.m. Central Time).

Endpapers *Goldfinger*'s Shirley Eaton,
1964. *Photographs by Loomis Dean*
Page 1 "James Bond" escorts
Queen Elizabeth II to the Olympics
Opening Ceremonies in July 2012.
*Photograph courtesy The Royal
Household © Crown Copyright*
Pages 2–3 Bond's Aston Martin.
Photograph by Michael Cole/Corbis
These pages Sean Connery, not dead.
Photograph from Bettmann/Corbis

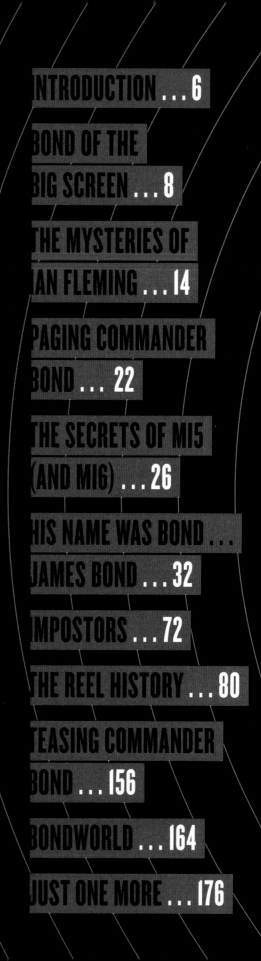

50 YEARS OF JAMES BOND

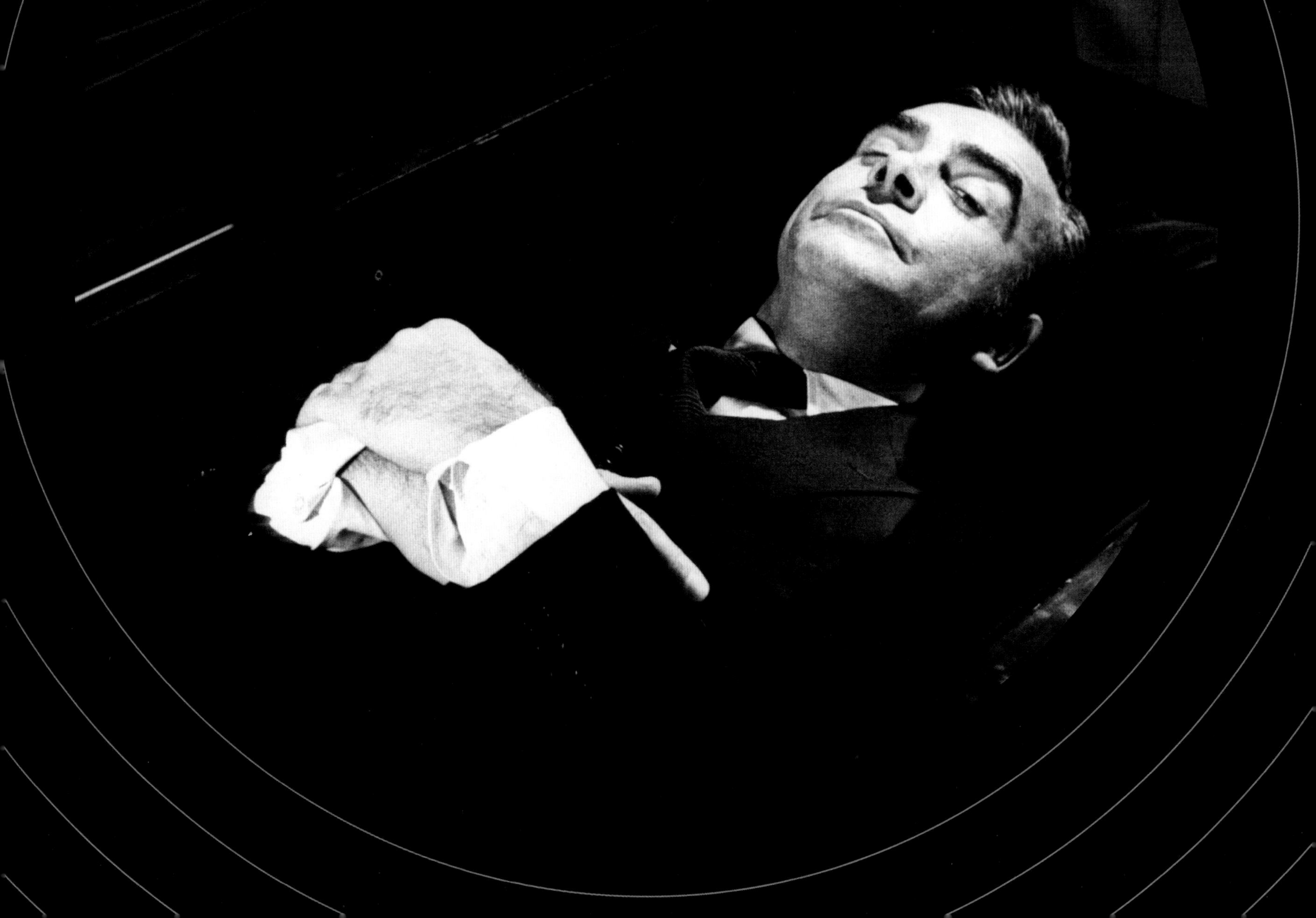

HAPPY ANNIVERSARY COMMANDER BOND

Sean has aged, Roger has aged, Pierce has aged, and even Daniel has aged a bit. James has not.

James Bond is back. It's a slogan as old as 1963, when the second film in the famous series, *From Russia with Love,* opened, and it is being voiced again to welcome *Skyfall* to your neighborhood IMAX. Bond fans, of which you are one, exult, and others marvel that the superspy is still with us: 50 years after *Dr. No* opened, 23 movies in all. (Well, not *quite* all, as will be explained in our pages: There were two "unofficial" feature films made, plus a television adaptation of a Bond novel, *Casino Royale,* that aired way back in 1954.)

Twenty-three (or 25, or 26) movies; six (or seven, or eight) James Bonds; 50 years-plus . . .

And 007 is still walking into M's office every couple of years and accepting his assignment, which usually amounts to saving a good chunk of the civilized world.

Let's be clear: James Bond and the Broccoli family, which continues to oversee the franchise, did not invent the notion of a film series. There were 27 Rin Tin Tin movies, mostly in the 1920s and '30s; 47 Charlie Chans from 1926 through 1949; 14 Sherlock

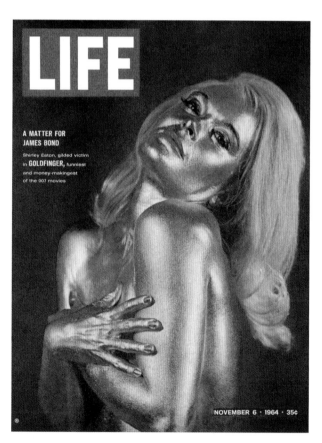

A MATTER FOR JAMES BOND

Shirley Eaton, gilded victim in **GOLDFINGER,** funniest and money-makingest of the 007 movies

NOVEMBER 6 · 1964 · 35¢

Holmeses starring Basil Rathbone; 16 Dr. Kildares in the 1930s and '40s; 16 Andy Hardys; 48 Bowery Boys films in the '40s and '50s; half a dozen or more Mothras and 29 Godzillas (including a few Mothra-Godzilla smack-downs) beginning in 1954. Since 1949, also in Asia, there have been 89 movies made involving Wong Fei-hung, a Chinese folk hero. Bond, who has caught so many characters through the years, will never catch Wong Fei-hung.

But Bond, it can be said, is largely responsible for the big-budget IMAX installments, offshoots and reboots we see today: the latest *X-Men, Madagascar, Ice Age, Batman, Superman, Spider-Man, Toy Story, Star Wars, Harry Potter* or J.R.R. Tolkien entry. We have been subjected to a dozen *Friday the 13th* and/or Jason and/or Freddy movies, including a 2009 reboot. It is expected that, if the money looked right, Stallone would reappear as Rocky or Rambo (he's done so as recently as 2006 and '08). As he has nothing filming, the money must not look right.

James Bond has made money from the get-go and is in fine fiscal health today. He is also in fine physical fettle as interpreted by Daniel Craig, the most impressively chiseled (if shortest) actor to assume the role. *Skyfall* is Craig's third go-round as 007, and the first two editions of this tougher, grittier Bond, *Casino Royale* and *Quantum of Solace*, have been embraced not only by the fandom but by critics—hardly the usual case in Bond's long and aesthetically checkered history. The Oscar-winning director Sam Mendes is helming *Skyfall*, and expectations are high. It is hoped the movie is a fitting capstone to Bond's anniversary year. We're sure it will be.

Assembling this commemorative book has been, for the editors of LIFE, nothing but pure, nostalgic fun. Our weekly magazine was in its heyday when Sean Connery's Bond bowed 50 years ago, and of course our staff back then paid attention, as the covers on these pages illustrate. All three of these pictures—of *Goldfinger*'s Shirley Eaton, of Connery, and of Bond's creator, the British writer Ian Fleming—were made by staff photographer Loomis Dean, who was our man on the Bond Beat in the days when Bond and the Beatles were just about the biggest things in the world. Reviewing Loomis's images all these years later, including many that didn't run in our pages at the time, brought us back to the excitement of those days.

Then we traveled through the eras: Lazenby (well, hardly an era), Moore, Dalton (not much of an era), Brosnan, Craig. We watched each of them grow in the role—and a few of them, in particular Connery and Moore, grow a bit too old in the role.

We asked ourselves: What else would our Bond-fan readers want? And so

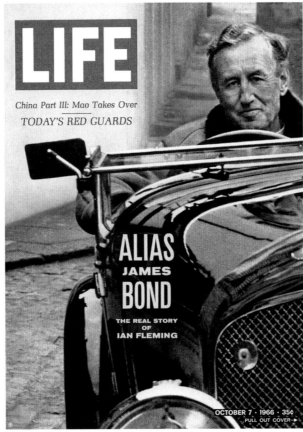

Maxwell Smart, Napoleon Solo (invented by Ian Fleming, by the way), Johnny English, Harry Palmer and April Dancer are in these pages as well. Of course there is all the behind-the-scenes stuff: Fleming at home, and a look at who he really was and how his fiction was informed by his wartime role in British intelligence; Shirley Eaton getting painted for her once-in-a-lifetime scene (in which, of course, she's dead); Connery napping between takes during the making of *Diamonds Are Forever*, when perhaps he should have been making milder fare than James Bond.

We piled on the fun facts that film aficionados love—Bond Girl lore and legend, all of those cool toys supplied by Q. But we also thought: We need context. And so we went to our friend Richard Corliss, the esteemed film critic, who has watched Bond all the way through for *Time* magazine, and asked him to explain what it was all about. Fifty years, after all. How did that happen? Does Bond represent something more than, well, just entertainment and escapism? Or is that quite enough? Richard's insightful, fun essay begins on the very next page.

Fifty years ago or 25 or even 10, when the new version of *Casino Royale* was yet to open, we never could have anticipated doing this book. But now, having seen Bond dodge so many bullets and give all of us so much pleasure, we're not betting against a centennial volume celebrating the next few dozen films. It seems James Bond will be with us always, and we can assure you: LIFE will be, too.

BOND OF THE BIG SCREEN

The first thought was to change Ian Fleming's spy into a woman, but Bond dodged an early bullet. By Richard Corliss

The air is electric at this posh London casino. A beautiful woman has been losing big at chemin de fer. How can the stranger across the table keep drawing better cards out of the shoe? Desperately, she borrows more to cover her bets, and the stranger says, "I admire your courage, Miss . . ."

"Trench," the brunette answers. "Sylvia Trench." She appraises her rival with an envy edging toward lust. "I admire your luck, Mr. . . . ."

"Bond." The silver cigarette lighter snaps shut to reveal a face of elegant cruelty: dimples welded like scars, incredible long whips of eyebrows, a full mouth ready for any challenge—to spit out a witticism, to commandeer a kiss, to sip from the cup of revenge. To say his name: "James Bond."

Moviegoers first heard that terse exchange in a London theater on October 5, 1962. That same week, Johnny Carson became host of *The Tonight Show*, and Pope John XXIII adorned the cover of *Time*. In two weeks, Khrushchev and Kennedy would go eyeball to eyeball in a dispute over Cuban missiles. So who cared about the world premiere of *Dr. No*, the first film made from Ian Fleming's James Bond novels, or about the introduction of Sean Connery as Her Majesty's hunkiest secret servant? Who knew?

Fifty years later—also nine Presidents, four popes, two *Tonight Show* hosts and some 2,500 issues of *Time*—the Soviet Union has disappeared, depriving the West of its longtime world threat, and Bond of a favorite nemesis. The entertainment landscape has changed, as most people see movies on home video or personal computers. Fleming himself died in 1964, having written 12 Bond novels and eight short stories. Yet the Bond films abide, in movie theaters, on DVD and as spin-off animated series and video games.

Before sequels became the most reliable way to make a buck, Bond set the standard for lavish serial adventures. Before Hollywood found gold in big-budget

adaptations of comic-book sagas—in the *Superman*, *Batman* and *Spider-Man* blockbusters—Bond was the movies' first franchise superhero. Spanning fully half a century of feature films, Bond is also the longest-running continuous English-language movie series. Things change, including the actors who play him, but Bond goes on saving the world from megalomaniac crime masters, heartless femmes fatales and indifferently prepared vodka martinis.

This multimedia legend has also weathered many changes of leading actors. Bond was first played on American television, in a 48-minute adaptation of *Casino Royale* on the 1954 anthology series *Climax!*, by Barry Nelson. (Peter Lorre was the villainous Le Chiffre.) In the 1967 spoof version of the same novel, at least six actors—David Niven, Peter Sellers and Ursula Andress among them—laid claim to being 007.

But in the official Bond films supervised by Harry Saltzman and Albert R. "Cubby" Broccoli, and then by Barbara Broccoli and Michael G. Wilson, so far, there have been a half dozen: Connery in six films (*Dr. No*, *From Russia with Love*, *Goldfinger*, *Thunderball*, *You Only Live Twice* and *Diamonds Are Forever*, plus the "unofficial" *Never Say Never Again*), the Australian model George Lazenby in *On Her Majesty's Secret Service*, Roger Moore in seven (*Live and Let Die*, *The Man with the Golden Gun*, *The Spy Who Loved Me*, *Moonraker*, *For Your Eyes Only*, *Octopussy* and *A View to a Kill*), Timothy Dalton in two (*The Living Daylights* and *Licence to Kill*), Pierce Brosnan in four (*GoldenEye*, *Tomorrow Never Dies*, *The World Is Not Enough* and *Die Another Day*), and Daniel Craig in, so far, three (*Casino Royale*, *Quantum of Solace* and the new *Skyfall*).

Bond is a 50-year family business: Barbara Broccoli is Cubby's daughter, Wilson his stepson. And over the decades, the creative team has remained remarkably consistent. Richard Maibaum wrote or cowrote 13 of the first 16 films; Neal Purvis and Robert Wade have written or

Now....meet the most extraordinary gentleman spy in all fiction.........

JAMES BOND
Agent 007...

007

THE FIRST JAMES BOND FILM ADVENTURE!

IAN FLEMING'S

Dr. No

007 THE DOUBLE "O" MEANS HE HAS A LICENSE TO KILL WHEN HE CHOOSES...WHERE HE CHOOSES....WHOM HE CHOOSES!

cowritten the last five. Composer John Barry, production designer Ken Adam and Maurice Binder, who created the swirling opening-credits sequences, stayed with the franchise for a generation or more.

Directors have been chosen usually from the middle rank of the British pack; the Broccolis, who run this producers' franchise, haven't followed the trend of Marvel comics movies, where quirky auteurs like Sam Raimi and Joss Whedon stamp their personalities on blockbuster projects. When they needed a new man behind the megaphone, the Broccolis would often promote from within: editor Peter Hunt, second-unit director John Glen. This familiar loyalty extends to the supporting cast. Only three actors (Bernard Lee, Robert Brown and Judi Dench) have played Bond's spy boss M; only three (Desmond Llewelyn, John Cleese and now Ben Whishaw in the new *Skyfall*) have played the gadgetmaster Q. If actors are replaced, it's often because they're deceased.

The series is big business too. The first 22 Broccoli Bonds have earned something like $5 billion around the world. (Broccoli did not produce the 1967 *Casino Royale*—the team would finally film that property in 2006—or Connery's freelance return to the role in the aforementioned 1983 *Never Say Never Again*.) In "real dollars," the series has earned much more; the 1965 *Thunderball* took in today's equivalent of more than a billion all by itself. Nor has the series suffered a slump in audience esteem: Each of the last five installments has, before adjustment, grossed more at the North American box office than its predecessor. The tap keeps flowing with the October release of the 23rd episode, *Skyfall*, which, along with 007's Olympic appearance, serves as the capstone of a year celebrating the Bond movies' golden jubilee.

HOW BOND WON THE COLD WAR

Money's nice, and if Bond hadn't made a bundle he wouldn't still be around. But the true measure of the franchise is its cultural and political impact. Begun in the deep freeze of the Cold War, as the world suffered its worst case of nuclear nerves, the Bond films lifted grim reality airborne into wish-fulfillment. It

could almost be said that this fictional British spy changed the world as much as any actual secret agent. The great Soviet bear had missiles and tractors; the Anglo-American alliance had missiles—and James Bond.

Any actual British Secret Service operative in 1962, a year after the Berlin Wall went up, might have been underground in the U.S.S.R. or the German Democratic Republic, matching wits and fists with members of the Soviet spy syndicate SMERSH (a Russian acronym for "Death of Spies"). The agency figures importantly in three of Fleming's first five Bond novels: *Casino Royale, Live and Let Die* and *From Russia with Love* (even though the real-world organization had technically dissolved in 1946). Yet SMERSH is mentioned in just two of the Broccoli Bond films, *From Russia with Love* and the 1987 *The Living Daylights* (and in the 1967 non-Broccoli *Casino Royale*). In the entire Bond canon, only one scene is set at the Berlin Wall—at the beginning of the 1983 *Octopussy*, released six years before that Cold War fixture crumbled. Otherwise, Bond left the grittier aspects of British spying to the films made from John le Carré and Len Deighton novels.

That was fine with the Broccolis, who always had sharp business instincts. They realized that, with a worldwide audience lapping up the franchise, it would be fiscally irresponsible to write off the whole communist world by casting Soviets as bad guys. So Bond found villains in rogue warriors, not cold warriors. In six of the first seven installments, Bond grapples with the international conspiracy known as SPECTRE (SPecial Executive for Counterintelligence, Terrorism, Revenge and Extortion), a clear inspiration for the League of Shadows in Christopher Nolan's recent Batman films. Throughout the Bond series, the U.S.S.R. remained an irrelevance, occasionally a gruff ally. Indeed, in *A View to a Kill*—released in 1985, two years before Ronald Reagan went to Berlin and challenged Mikhail Gorbachev to "Tear down this wall!"—"Comrade Bond" was awarded the Order of Lenin.

"Make no mistake," real-life U.S. secret agent Valerie Plame wrote in *Variety*, "Bond is an assassin, as his special '00' code indicates. His job isn't to form relationships, it's to end them." Yet in the permanent fantasy land of popular entertainment, this assassin gave the traditional action hero modern attitudes and equipment. He brought a killer's lightning instincts to Sherlock Holmes, a suave caress to crude Mike Hammer, the microchip age to Dick Tracy's gadgets. His films were comic strips with grown-up cynicism, Hitchcock thrillers without the artistic risks.

Bond, especially Connery's Bond, was an existential hired gun with an aristocrat's tastes—just right for a time when class was a matter of brand names and insouciant gestures. "My dear girl," Bond tells a new conquest in the 1964 *Goldfinger*, "there are some things that just aren't done. Such as drinking Dom Perignon '53 above a temperature of 38 degrees Fahrenheit. That's as bad as listening to the Beatles without earmuffs." Minutes later the dear girl's body is lacquered to death by Auric Goldfinger's Korean manservant. But death doesn't shake Bond's assurance in his infallibility—or in his mandarin musical prejudice against the other great British export of the 1960s.

To an empire that had seen its realm shrink with the loss of the Indian subcontinent, and its secret service embarrassed by the Cambridge Five and Profumo scandals, the notion of an agent from the U.K. saving the free world was an intoxicating tonic. Britain mattered. Britain was cool. (And the U.S., as epitomized by Bond's CIA ally Felix Leiter, was just a sidekick.) If the Beatles made England swing for the young, then Bond was a travel-poster boy for the earmuff brigade. The Bond films even put a few theme songs, such as Paul McCartney's "Live and Let Die," on the pop charts. As we will see, sometimes hilariously, in these pages: In its first flush of fame, the Bond series spawned a whole genre of superspy imitators—Matt Helm and Harry Palmer in '60s movies, Maxwell Smart and the men and girls from U.N.C.L.E. on TV. The Beatles shot some of their second movie,

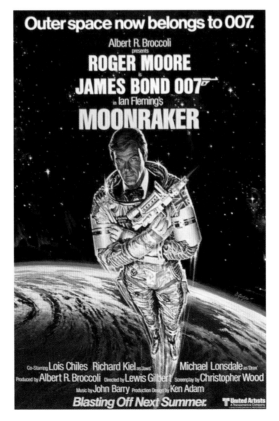

Help!, in the Bahamas partly because they heard that the latest Bond film, *Thunderball*, was going there for location work. The upstarts were following the big boy.

Later a young generation of filmmakers found inspiration in the series' success. You hear its echoes in hundreds of high-tech adventure movies, from *Star Wars* (with Darth Vader as a more sepulchral Dr. No) and *Raiders of the Lost Ark* (007 as an archaeologist) up to *The Dark Knight Rises* (superhero vs. maniacal, aphorism-spouting villain). Some of the influence was direct: John Stears, the effects wizard of *Star Wars*, supervised the visual tricks on six early Bonds. Other directors learned just by watching, as enthralled kids who grew up to bring their own spin to the brut effervescence and special-effects expertise bottled in Bond.

THE BOND WOMEN

James Bond could have been Jane Bond. In 1955, not long after the publication of *Casino Royale*, the Russian-born producer-director Gregory Ratoff optioned the book and hired the young Lorenzo Semple Jr. (who later did the screenplay for *Never Say Never Again*) to write a script. Neither man thought much of the main character. "Frankly, we thought he was kind of unbelievable and as I recall, even kind of stupid," Semple recalled in *Variety*. "So Gregory thought the solution was to make Bond a woman, 'Jane Bond' if you will, and he even had a plan to cast Susan Hayward in the role." The notion of a top dramatic actress from Brooklyn to play the veddy British, Type-A male 007 came to naught, and a few years later Harry Saltzman snagged the rights to most of Fleming's Bond books.

As the first two decades of Bond films made celebrities of his enemies (Oddjob, Rosa Klebb, Ernst Stavro Blofeld, Jaws), so they incited schoolboy snickers with the names of his women. Pussy Galore and Octopussy! Kissy Suzuki and Plenty O'Toole! Mary Goodnight and Holly Goodhead! They were as indispensable and interchangeable as 007's other accessories, the Walther PPK and the Aston Martin. In the early '60s the Fleming books enjoyed a boost in popularity when President Kennedy sang their praises in LIFE magazine. The endorsement was apt, for Bond in the early Connery years comprised equal parts Jack Kennedy's playboy glamour and Hugh Hefner's Playboy Philosophy.

In that man's-man's world, women were to be valued as playmates, as allies or adversaries, and mostly as ornaments. *Goldfinger*'s Pussy Galore (Honor Blackman) might be a judo expert who could toss Bond like a crepe, but he would pin her with a wolfish double entendre: "We must have a few fast falls together sometime." Or, as he says when his bed time with another *Goldfinger* lovely, Jill Masterson (Shirley Eaton), is interrupted by an urgent phone call from Leiter, "No, look, I'm sorry. I can't. Something big's come up." Back in 1964, Bond's allusion to his tumescent member earned a gasp or a giggle. That suited 007's suave satyriasis; recall that most films gave him two "Bond Girls" (the blonde, the brunette) to tangle with. The playboy would enjoy his sport with them and move on.

His roving eye was in part a function of a spy's globe-trotting itinerary. Other movie superheroes could form lasting domestic partnerships—Superman/Clark Kent with Lois Lane, Batman/Bruce Wayne with Rachel Dawes—because they lived and worked in one city (Metropolis, Gotham). For all their preternatural skills, they were tethered to their jobs as, respectively, reporter and philanthropist: essentially working stiffs. Bond was always working, and often stiff, but his jet-set escapades virtually demanded

UNITED ARTISTS/EVERETT (3)

that he get in bed with the enemy. That job requirement would put a crimp in any affair back home with, say, Miss Moneypenny.

Yet, even at the start, the Bond Girl was as clever, efficient and often as ruthless in combat as she was exciting in bed—a Jane Bond, if you will. And though the series never merited a citation from *Ms.* magazine, it gradually insinuated a certain sly feminism. Bond was still susceptible to European beauties of no fixed abode or accent, but he began to rely on their intelligence and independence. They could fight manfully; he could fall in love. He married one of them, Contessa Teresa di Vicenzo (Diana Rigg) in *On Her Majesty's Secret Service*, which of course meant she had to die violently.

More than a few Bond girls had the IQ and skills set to match his: ace pilot and former CIA operative Pam Bouvier (Carey Lowell) in *Licence to Kill;* rocket scientist, also ex-CIA, Holly Goodhead (Lois Chiles) in *Moonraker;* nuclear physicist Dr. Christmas Jones (Denise Richards) in *The World Is Not Enough.* Some overage boys could drool as Andress emerged from the sea like Aphrodite in a bikini in the 1962 *Dr. No,* or 40 years later when Halle Berry reprised that scene in *Die Another Day.* But others could cheer the high kung-fu kicks of Michelle Yeoh's Wai Lin in *Tomorrow Never Dies,* or lose their hearts to Eva Green's Vesper Lynd in the 2006 reboot of *Casino Royale.*

WHO IS JAMES BOND?

Ask Bond-watchers of a certain age about the six actors who have slipped into Bond's Savile Row suits in the Broccoli franchise, and they might say it's really Connery and five other guys—since he, being first and being Sean, stamped the role with his sulfurous masculinity. When Connery tired of the role (and it showed), Broccoli and Saltzman cast Lazenby in the installment where Bond became a husband

and a widower. In the game of casting roulette, it was Lazenby who disappeared as Connery returned for one more film.

Then Moore took over for seven episodes. Amiable and reliable, he nonetheless walked through his part like a waxwork on casters, like Bond embalmed, and left most of the heavy work to stunt doubles. The best of his films, *The Spy Who Loved Me,* succeeded without serious intervention from its star. Most of the other Moore Bonds were bloated fantasies, heavy on the double entendres; the series was in danger of becoming a travelogue with gadgets and a smirk.

Depending on the actor, portrayals of 007 have alternated between Rough Bond and Smooth Bond. Dalton, a West End stage luminary with heartthrob looks, played Bond with the ironic scowl of a killer who is battle-ready yet war-weary. Dalton did a lot of his own stunts, and he cut a smart figure in a tuxedo—especially the one with the Velcro lapels, in *The Living Daylights,* that could fold over to give him the guise of a priest-assassin. But he seemed to be performing under protest, and after two films he broke out of Bondage and returned to the stage.

Paging a Smooth Bond: the puckish Irishman Brosnan, who imported his blithe persona from the *Remington Steele* series. Radiating TV-star warmth rather than movie-star heat, Brosnan escorted the series into late middle age, through the 2002 *Die Another Day.* Still immensely popular, the Bond films had become increasingly irrelevant, a chipper anachronism in a decade of tortured heroes from comic books (Nolan's *Batman Begins*) and spy fiction (Matt Damon's films as the amnesiac secret agent Jason Bourne).

BOND REDUX

Bond needed a makeover, and got it in the 2006 *Casino Royale.* The movie showed a perfect figure rising from the sea—lubricated and lubricious, like Ursula Andress in

Dr. No—but this body belonged not to any Bond enchantress but to Daniel Craig, with Sisyphus shoulders and pecs so well defined they could be in *Webster's.* If Craig spent more time with his shirt off than all previous Bonds combined, it was to make the point that this secret agent was his own sex object. In any romance he had with a shady lady, he seemed to be cheating on himself.

Figuring that modern audiences preferred murderous fights to martini-sipping, the Broccoli brain trust made Craig's 007 a working-class bloke, as much thug as thinker. Instead of the 007 of the Fleming canon—a tough but smooth gentleman spy, schooled at Eton and Cambridge—Craig is nearly a cyber- or cipher-Bond, with a loyalty chip implanted in a mechanism that's built for murderous ingenuity. In lieu of the bons mots assigned to Connery, Moore and Brosnan, Craig communicates in grunts and sullen, conceivably soulful, laser stares. For this 007, spying is no game; it's work, a job that has become a compulsion. Craig's 007 is a brute: Rambo in a tux and, even more so, a Bourne-again Bond.

Rather than losing faith in the traditional Bond by jolting 007 into gritty modernism, the Broccoli team is simply showing the adaptability that has sustained the series for a half century. The Craig Bond might in fact be what the Connery Bond would have been if the franchise had started from scratch now. Movie heroes no longer sit in tuxedos and smoke cigarettes at a chemin-de-fer table; the fights are longer and more vicious; and every entendre is single. The Broccolis were right to bring 007 into the 21st century, rather than serve as curators of the James Bond Museum. After all, that archive is kept faithfully in the memories of millions of fans—and in the bright and lively pages of this jubilee book.

THE MYSTERIES OF
IAN FLEMING

Was the creator of the character the man who would be Bond, or was Bond the man who would be Fleming?

t has been said: Many millions of men around the world have wanted to be James Bond. Ian Fleming was the first.

That's as it should be, of course; he had ownership rights. Quite literally, Bond was Fleming's baby, born of nothing but his febrile imagination. From the first, Fleming formed his fictional hero in his own self-image, and wasn't shy about this even as he was also happy to cultivate a certain air of mystery. He was one of a few successful British male authors including Graham Greene and John le Carré (the latter of whom will not like being lumped with Fleming and has voiced a strong distaste for Bond) who wrote exclusively or occasionally about espionage; who were happy to acknowledge that their own past histories in wartime intelligence informed their fiction; and who were good-looking guys, not shy in front of a camera. Many of the best portraits of Fleming have the ubiquitous cigarette smoke swirling in a frame around his handsome face, his fixed gaze encouraging the question: Who is this man? Is he James Bond?

In certain essentials, yes, yes he was.

Both Ian and James were, to return to those photographs, chain smokers—Fleming worse even than Bond, who early in the first novel lights his 17th cigarette of the day (Fleming reportedly enjoyed four times that many in a typical day). Both liked to drink, certainly too heavily. Both were attractive to women, and both were womanizers. If Fleming calmed down (somewhat) after his marriage in 1952 at age 43 to Anne Geraldine Charteris, it can be noted that it was his affair with Anne that led to her divorce from Viscount Rothermere. Bond, too, had occasion to sleep with married women.

This kind of symbiosis goes further back. M (well, Fleming, writing as M) submitted an obituary of Bond to *The Times* of London in *You Only Live Twice*, and many holes were filled in. Bond's birthdate was never given (perhaps in a moment of self-loathing, Fleming once awarded his own birthdate, May 28, 1908, to the arch-criminal Ernst Stavro Blofeld), but it was said that Bond had lied about his age in order to qualify for active service in World War II; this, coupled with a passing reference to retirement age in *Moonraker*, would peg Bond to be of a younger generation than Fleming's, born sometime in the 1920s. Valentine Fleming, Ian's father, was killed in action during World War I when the boy was 9; Bond's parents both died in a climbing accident when he was young. Bond and Fleming attended Eton and excelled at schoolboy athletics (Fleming, however, was not expelled for a sexual liaison

with an Eton maid). Bond's height (six feet), hairstyle and eye color are the same as Fleming's.

The most interesting parallels have always been based upon Fleming's career during World War II, which drew him and his fictional counterpart into the world of British Military Intelligence. We will learn something about Britain's MI agencies a few pages on, but for now: Fleming rose to the rank of lieutenant commander in the Royal Naval Volunteer Reserve (as would Bond) and worked directly, and admirably, for the director of Naval Intelligence. His so-called Trout Memo, which urged a fly-fishing deception method, was instrumental in the successful Operation Mincemeat of 1943.

ON THE PREVIOUS PAGES and on these two, Fleming adopts suitable poses for a successful writer of espionage thrillers—all photographs taken circa 1960. He is at this point in time known as James Bond's author, and more than two-thirds of the oeuvre has been written, but Bond is still several months away from his debut on the big screen.

LOOMIS DEAN

EVERETT

EVENING STANDARD/GETTY

LOOMIS DEAN

LOOMIS DEAN

THE TIMES/NI SYNDICATION (2)

LOOMIS DEAN

"A Suggestion (not a very nice one)," was how Fleming headlined his memorandum. "The following suggestion is used in a book by Basil Thomson: a corpse dressed as an airman, with dispatches in his pockets, could be dropped on the coast, supposedly from a parachute that has failed. I understand there is no difficulty in obtaining corpses at the Naval Hospital, but, of course, it would have to be a fresh one." Fleming was also in charge of Operation Golden Eye, an intelligence and sabotage initiative in Spain, and of No. 30 Commando unit (also known as Assault Unit 30), an intelligence–gathering military unit. He consulted on T-Force, whose operations greatly informed the action in the third Bond novel, 1955's *Moonraker*.

THE LIFE AS LIVED, and as portrayed: On this page, at left, Fleming is seen with his wife, Anne (top), and son, Caspar (below). Theirs was not a solid family unit; Anne considered her husband's writing "cheap pornography"; he would not attend her dinner parties; neither paid attention to their son, who was shuffled off to boarding schools. Caspar was discovered with a cache of guns during his years at Eton, dropped out of Oxford and died by his own hand in 1975. Ian Fleming was self-absorbed and career oriented, whether posing for LIFE with handguns (top right) or fancy cars (opposite) to further the Bond legend, contributing information during the war to the director of Naval Intelligence (above, center) or working for the *Times*. Above, right: A non-bylined piece by foreign correspondent Fleming in 1939.

During World War II, Fleming confided that one day he hoped to write a spy novel. He was certainly gathering the goods. "[Bond] was a compound of all the secret agents and commandos I met during the war," he later acknowledged. Foremost, besides himself, were his older and revered brother Peter, who was instrumental in behind-the-lines ops in Norway and Greece (and who would go on to be a noted travel writer, his literary career preceding Ian's); Conrad O'Brien-ffrench, a skiing spy; Patrick Dalzel-Job of No. 30 Commando; and Wilfred "Biffy" Dunderdale of the MI6 office in Paris, a man of great charm given to handmade suits, fine cufflinks and Rolls-Royces.

So Fleming, who took jobs in journalism in the postwar years, had the stuff of James Bond, but not yet the impetus. That arrived early in 1952 when he and Anne, who was pregnant, agreed to marry. To relieve tension, Fleming took to the desk at his Goldeneye estate in Jamaica and wrote *Casino Royale* in little more than two months.

Fleming lived long enough to author 14 books, to enjoy some of Bond's success (but not the über-celebrity that would follow the *Goldfinger* and then *Thunderball* movies) and to shore up the notion that he was Bond. Fleming loved to travel, and all Bond novels except *Moonraker* featured travel; he loved Jamaica, and *Live and Let Die*, *Dr. No* and *The Man with the Golden Gun* have settings there; he loved cars; he loved golf, and his Royal St. George's Golf Club in Sandwich, Kent, is certainly the model for Royal St. Mark's, where Bond and Goldfinger duel; he loved skiing and the Alps, and these are integral in *On Her Majesty's Secret Service;* he loved snorkeling and scuba diving, and there, then, is *Thunderball;* he loved bridge, and Bond bests Sir Hugo Drax in *Moonraker;* he loved scrambled eggs, and Bond, epicure though he is, does too.

There was a history of heart disease in Fleming's family—plus there were all those cigarettes smoked and cocktails imbibed over the years—and he suffered his first major heart attack in 1962 at 53 years of age. He was never the same, and was stricken again at the Royal St. George's Golf Club on August 12, 1964—the 12th birthday of his son, Caspar. (A decade on, tragically, Caspar would take his own life.) Fleming would die at the hospital, but en route he said to the ambulance drivers, "I am sorry to trouble you chaps. I don't know how you get along so fast with the traffic on the roads these days." The eternally composed James Bond might have said the same.

DAVE G. HOUSER/CORBIS

HARRY BENSON

HIS GOLDENEYE RETREAT in Oracabessa on the north shore of Jamaica meant everything to Fleming, and was where just about all of the Bond prose was fashioned—when the dogs would leave him be. He had bought the property atop a cliff and built his three-bedroom house before fame overtook him; there he enjoyed hosting his many friends from the cultural and political worlds. He said at one point that he named the estate in tribute to Carson McCullers's novel *Reflections in a Golden Eye* and at another point to Operation Golden Eye, with which he had been affiliated during the war. The name was never used by him for a Bond novel, but was the title of the first film starring Pierce Brosnan as 007 in 1995. Twelve years after Fleming died in 1964, reggae star Bob Marley looked into buying the estate, but it was ultimately sold to his friend Chris Blackwell, the music mogul and producer. Fleming used to enjoy Goldeneye's private beach. Today, the adjacent James Bond Beach, where Ursula Andress once filmed scenes for *Dr. No,* is known for its two-story Moonraker bar and its annual music concerts and festivals, which have featured such stars as Bob's son Ziggy Marley and Rihanna.

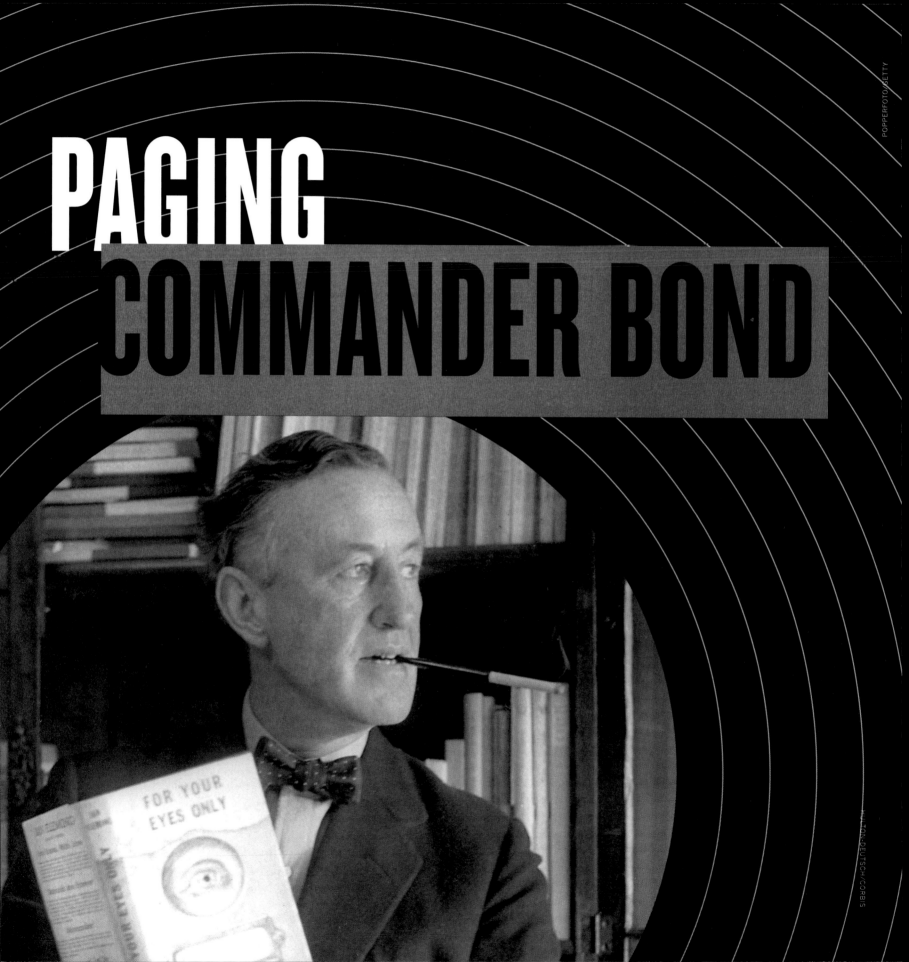

PAGING
COMMANDER BOND

FOR YOUR
EYES ONLY

This year actually marks 59 years of James Bond, who lived in books well before he hit the big screen.

As recently mentioned, Ian Fleming was feeling the heat of impending matrimony and so, as a distraction, he closeted himself in Jamaica and cast his mind back to his days in the intelligence service. It took him three tries to get the first sentence of *Casino Royale* right. "Scent and smoke and sweat hit the taste buds . . ." yielded to "Scent and smoke and sweat can suddenly combine together and hit the taste buds with an acid shock . . ." and this was rightly refined to "The scent and smoke and sweat of a casino are nauseating at three in the morning." That sentence done, it was off to the races. Fleming reportedly began the book on January 15, 1952, and, hammering out 2,000 words a day on his Imperial typewriter, finished it on March 18, 1952. He showed it to a member of his alumnae association of former girlfriends, who recommended that, if he publish it at all, he employ a pseudonym. Maybe that's why she was an ex-girlfriend.

Undeterred at age 43, he sent the manuscript along to William Plomer, the South African novelist, poet and librettist, who recommended it to the publishers Jonathan Cape. They said yes and printed a modest first run. Nearly 5,000 copies were sold in Britain within a month, and James Bond was in the conversation. The novel did not do well in the United States, but it would eventually. Plomer went on to edit several of the Bond books (12 novels; two collections) that his friend would write at a pace of one a year until his death in 1964.

There are some key points to be made about the Fleming output, particularly as it evolved in the early years. At first, James Bond was almost a small-shop, even quaint enterprise; Ian Fleming himself was allowed to design the original dust jacket for *Casino Royale,* seen above. There was no effort made by his publishers or editors to have him sex up the actions or attitudes of his heroic, relatively humorless and often conflicted spy (Bond seriously contemplates not only marriage but early retirement in the first book). They didn't even have Fleming sex up the name. "When I wrote the first one in 1953, I wanted Bond to be an extremely dull, uninteresting man to

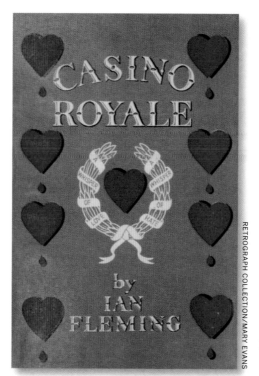

RETROGRAPH COLLECTION/MARY EVANS

whom things happened; I wanted him to be a blunt instrument," he told *The New Yorker* in 1962. "When I was casting around for a name for my protagonist I thought, by God, [that] is the dullest name I ever heard." The name belonged to an American ornithologist whose authoritative *Birds of the West Indies* was on the table at Fleming's Goldeneye estate. "It struck me that this brief, unromantic, Anglo-Saxon and yet very masculine name was just what I needed, and so a second James Bond was born," Fleming later told the ornithologist's wife, by way of explanation if not apology.

Fleming continued in his job at the *Sunday Times,* where he was foreign manager, often pumping his correspondents for details about exotic locales that might freshen his fiction. He produced the novels at Goldeneye: "[W]hile I still do a certain amount of the writing in the midst of my London life, it is on my annual visits to Jamaica that all of my books have been written." It should be noted that Fleming's fiction was written before the mania set in and the movie image of Bond was firmly fixed. There was no pressure to make the spy wittier or more gadget-happy than Fleming saw him. For these reasons, the James Bond of the page is a different animal than the one on the big screen, but all the more intriguing for it.

There have been many "James Bond" novels written by others since Fleming's death, most of them in authorized editions. We do not discount them here—some are said to be very good—but we do not include them. There are more than 100 million copies of books starring Fleming's Bond floating around out there, in various stages of dog-eared-ness. They are the source material. They constitute the opus. They are the biography of Bond . . . James Bond.

ON THE PREVIOUS PAGES, the proud author poses with his books, including *On Her Majesty's Secret Service* and the 1960 short story collection *For Your Eyes Only,* which was largely adapted from unfilmed TV scripts and would go on to supply titles or partial plotlines to no fewer than four Bond films. On these pages, then and now: The very first dust jacket of the first Bond novel and (opposite) an exhibit of where Bond has gone since, at the Imperial War Museum in London.

MATT DUNHAM/AP

THE SECRETS OF MI5 (AND MI6)

British military intelligence agencies have long harbored superspies, double-agents and, interestingly, a bunch of best-selling writers in training.

The legendary name—the one embedded like an evil-doctor-implanted chip in the public's imagination and the conspiracy theorists' frontal lobes—is MI5 ("em-eye-five"), but that official designation hasn't existed for decades. It did once, though. It originally stood for Military Intelligence [Section] 5, which was a key unit of Great Britain's Secret Service Bureau, formed in 1909 to counter German espionage efforts. Section 5, or MI5, was renamed the Security Service in 1931, but the way-cool, spy-ish nomenclature lived on in the lingo, as did MI6, a later designation for the Secret Intelligence Service, which actually was an entirely separate organization dedicated to gathering information outside the United Kingdom (while MI5 was focused on protecting the kingdom internally). James Bond, according to the title of one of the books, was "On Her Majesty's Secret Service," which could have been either unit—but his activities strongly imply MI6. Anyway: Think of MI-whatever as the bowler-hatted version of the CIA, and you've got the picture. Ian Fleming was a member, and so was James Bond.

So were others, as the colorful and checkered history of the MIs, which is nearly as exciting as a Bond novel, tells us. There seems to have been a particular propensity for spying among the literati, and this shouldn't be surprising. Most of these people were smart and well-educated and, as patriotic Brits, would want to help the cause in dire times. W. Somerset Maugham was working for the Red Cross in France as an interpreter and medical assistant in World War I when he was approached by the Secret Intelligence Service; his novel *Of Human Bondage* had just been published, and the SIS figured his writerly career would be a good cover for his spying, while his fluency in German could be very useful. In the run-up to World War II, J.R.R. Tolkien was trained as a spy. Graham Greene traveled the world in search of subject matter for his fiction, and his peripatetic nature convinced his sister, Elisabeth, that he would be right for MI6, and she brought him in. During World War II he was posted to Sierra Leone, where his supervisor and friend was Kim Philby—to whom we'll return in just a moment. John le Carré, which is the pen name of David Cornwell, joined the British Army's Intelligence Corp in 1950, and two years later, while studying at Oxford, covertly worked for MI5 by spying on leftist organizations that might be harboring "commies."

Certainly some of them were—harboring or nurturing commies, that is. The most notorious scandal in British Secret Service history involved the so-called Cambridge Five, a ring of students who had been together at university in the 1930s and who later became double-agents for the Soviets. Greene's old running mate, Philby, was perhaps the most famous of the turncoats. He had been MI6, Anthony Blunt had been MI5, and they and their fellow communist sympathizers had all been active in intelligence units during World War II.

Britain's Secret Service survived that dark episode, and has even survived James Bond. Back in 1962, when it became known that Ian Fleming was on President Kennedy's list of favorite writers, *Izvestia,* the Soviets' press organ, bothered to deride the author and his creation, presumably to sully the reputation of U.S. and

RALPH CRANE

ON THE PREVIOUS PAGES: Some heretofore secret files are disseminated at the Public Record Office in Kew, West London. Above: David Cornwell, whose alias (well, whose nom de plume) is John le Carré, is happy enough to conspire in a publicity caper. Opposite: Film director Carol Reed (left) with Graham Greene. They have just finished collaborating on an adaptation of Greene's *The Third Man* and will team again on the film version of his wonderful satirical novel *Our Man in Havana,* a send-up of MI6.

LARRY BURROWS

British intelligence. *Time* magazine chuckled: "Soviet officialdom has good reason to fear Fleming's 'propaganda.' In no time, underprivileged Russian spymasters who read Bond's adventures will be demanding their own share of oversexed fillies and undercooked filets. Their expense accounts would wreck SMERSH more effectively than 007 himself."

And on November 15, 2006, when the Secret Intelligence Service allowed two anonymous operations officers to testify on BBC radio about the modern-day health of the organization, they said all was fine: There still was a Q-like figure dispersing technological toys, there still was a boss who went by a single letter (C, not M), there still was plenty of travel and adventure and skullduggery . . . But no, there was not now, nor had there ever been, a license to kill.

"WE'RE ALWAYS rubbing MI5 up the wrong way," Bond tells his CIA pal Felix Leiter in the novel *Live and Let Die.* "And they're always stepping on the corns of the Special Branch." The man from MI6 explains that this, the Special Branch, is Scotland Yard. On the opposite page, top left, is No. 21 Queen Anne's Gate in London, the office and residence of the head of MI6 when Bond would have been working there. The main office of Sir Stewart Menzies—the man who would have been M—was connected to the rest of the headquarters by a secret passageway. Then, right, is MI6 today at Vauxhall Cross in central London. Bottom: In an undated photograph taken in the Soviet Union sometime in the late 1960s are two men Bond would have dearly liked to get his hands on, Kim Philby (left) and George Blake. Both men were once MI6, and both were turncoats. Blake's story: He was convicted in 1961 of being a double-agent when evidence was presented that he had given the Soviets information on some 400 MI6 agents working in Germany in the 1950s (at least 42 KGB arrests of MI6 agents were pegged to Blake's duplicity). He escaped Wormwood Scrubs Prison in 1966 and made his way to the U.S.S.R., where he later broke bread with his brother rat Philby. Above: If any evidence besides educational pedigree were needed to illustrate the spies' aristocratic connections, here is Elizabeth II conferring with her personal art advisor, Sir Anthony Blunt, during a visit to the Courtauld Institute of Art of London University. In November 1979, Sir Anthony will be exposed as a Russian agent and, of course, stripped of his knighthood.

HIS NAME WAS BOND ...
JAMES BOND

SEAN CONNERY

GEORGE LAZENBY

BARRY NELSON

DAVID NIVEN

TIMOTHY DALTON

DANIEL CRAIG

ROGER MOORE

PIERCE BROSNAN

A million and more men dressed like, talked like, lit their cigarettes like and otherwise pretended to be just like James Bond. A lucky eight did so when the cameras were rolling, and thereby gained immortality.

HIS NAME WAS BOND… JIMMY BOND

Many modern cultural enterprises are laden with twists and turns in their histories that, once toted, add up to a trove of data as bounteous as it is delicious. Shirley Temple and other young women who were considered for the part of Dorothy—this is only the *beginning* of many fun facts to know and tell about *The Wizard of Oz.* And take the Beatles, for another instance: with those drummers in the closet (Pete Best, Jimmy Nicol and the studio guy, Andy White, on "Love Me Do") and Eric Clapton playing, uncredited, on "While My Guitar Gently Weeps."

So it is with the James Bond filmography, which, as we will learn in our trivia-barnacled book, has names attached to it ranging from Jack Lord to Orson Welles (both of whom appeared in Bond films) to Cary Grant to Clint Eastwood (neither of whom did, but might have—and as 007 himself).

A font of Bondiana is *Casino Royale,* first of the novels and, interestingly, first of the films, first among the satires (sacrilege!) and first of the recent reboots.

Really?

Yes, really.

You say, "No!"—meaning to indicate, of course, the good (well, bad, very bad) doctor. But we insist: Yes!

Dr. No was indeed the first feature-film release of a Bond movie, in 1962, but a full eight years earlier there had been a Bondian adaptation on American television.

Casino Royale has always been an outlier, and therefore a generator of trivia. The sole reason for this is: The march of Bond films through the years is hardly as crisp and disciplined as the heirs of Cubby Broccoli, guardians of the "official" canon, would have you believe. Ian Fleming's first book, published in 1953, was a hit in England, but in the United States it was barely noticed. Nevertheless, the producers of the CBS-TV anthology series *Climax!* secured the rights to produce a teleplay of *Casino Royale,* which aired in 1954, even eyeing the possibility of a spin-off James Bond series. After that, the rights of this novel traveled a path forever separate from the larger oeuvre that eventually was sold to the Canadian Harry Saltzman, who then partnered with Albert R. "Cubby" Broccoli in Eon Productions. This is why director John Huston was considering a *Casino Royale* movie in 1962 with the idea that Cary Grant would star; this is why there was that David Niven–Peter Sellers *Casino Royale* comedy in 1967; and this is why there was no "official" film until the Daniel Craig era, when MGM traded its partial rights to the Spider-Man franchise to Sony for the ability to finally film a "faithful" *Casino Royale.*

Not that the 48-minute teleplay that ran on TV on October 21, 1954, wasn't faithful enough. Goodness knows it tried hard, with a script cowritten by Charles Bennett, who had built a reputation in the 1930s in England writing the screenplays for several of director Alfred Hitchcock's early thrillers (*The Man Who Knew Too Much,*

EVERETT (2)

GAT IN HAND, Alan Baxter, who would go on to a successful career of hard-egg roles, confronts Barry Nelson (right) in the 1941 film *Shadow of the Thin Man,* Nelson's debut on the big screen. Thirteen years later, Nelson would hold the gun: as Jimmy Bond.

DOSSIER

NATIONALITY: American

BOND MOVIES: 1

AGE WHEN HE WAS BOND: 37

HAIR: Dark brown

EYES: Brown

HEIGHT: 5'11 ½"

PRIOR DISTINCTIONS: Paul Clarke in film debut, *Shadow of the Thin Man;* Broadway lead in Moss Hart plays

QUOTE: "I was scratching my head wondering how to play it. I hadn't read the book or anything like that because it wasn't well known."

NELSON CARVED OUT a career in an era when Hollywood prized versatility. Opposite: He is boyish between Donna Reed (left) and Myrna Loy, with the supine William Powell, in *Shadow of the Thin Man*. Top: One year later, in 1942, Nelson plays in a broader comedy, Bud Abbott (center) and Lou Costello's *Rio Rita*. Above: In 1963, he and Diana McBain bring *Mary, Mary* from the stage to the screen.

The 39 Steps, Secret Agent, Sabotage). We will learn more about the film itself, its faithfulness or lack thereof, on page 82.

For now, the ultimate trivia question: Who was the first James Bond? The answer is (drumroll, please . . .) Barry Nelson.

And why not? The nice-looking, tall-enough native San Franciscan was already a veteran of stage and screen by the time he was cast as Bond; he would have been familiar to most of the American TV audience.

Nelson began acting when still a teenager, continued at the University of California, Berkeley, and was signed by Metro-Goldwyn-Mayer soon after graduating in 1941. He made his film debut that same year in *Shadow of the Thin Man*, third-billed after William Powell and Myrna Loy, charismatic stars of the popular series, which was based on Dashiell Hammett's final novel, *The Thin Man*. (Trivia: What actor has hardboiled Hammett and Fleming in common? Barry Nelson!) In 1942, Nelson played opposite Robert Taylor and Lana Turner in the noir film *Johnny Eager*, then had the lead in the war movie *A Yank on the Burma Road*. Though an enlisted man in World War II, he found time to launch his Broadway career with a leading role in Moss Hart's *Winged Victory* in 1943. Five years later he would have a bigger success on the boards in Hart's *Light Up the Sky*, and he also starred with Barbara Bel Geddes in the original Broadway production of *The Moon Is Blue*.

The principal villain in *Casino Royale*—both novel and teleplay—is Le Chiffre, and when Nelson was told that the great Peter Lorre had signed to play the role, he was more than happy to take on Bond. But it wasn't James Bond, it was "Jimmy": the producers had asked Bennett to Americanize the story, and this meant, among other things, "Jimmy."

"At that time, no one had ever heard of James Bond," Nelson remembered in 2004 to *Cinema Retro* magazine. "I was scratching my head wondering how to play it."

The episode turned out to be a one-off, not a series pilot, and Nelson went on to a career of character parts (*Alfred Hitchcock Presents, Ben Casey, The Twilight Zone* on TV; the hotel manager who interviews Jack Nicholson for the caretaker's job in *The Shining*). He died in 2007 at age 86, not having finished the memoir that would have told us more about what it was like to originate James Bond.

By the way: The second Bond? Yes, on film, Sean Connery. But here's some more trivia: In 1956 the well-known British television and radio presenter Bob Holness assayed the role in a South African radio adaptation of *Moonraker*—the only known radio production of a Bond novel.

EVERETT (3)

DOSSIER

NATIONALITY: Scottish

BOND MOVIES: 7

AGE WHEN HE WAS BOND: 32–53

HAIR: Dark brown (already with a receding hairline, he wore a toupee for all of his Bond portrayals)

EYES: Brown

HEIGHT: 6'2"

PRIOR DISTINCTIONS: Veteran of the Royal Navy; contestant in the Mr. Universe contest

QUOTE: "I have always hated that damn James Bond. I'd like to kill him."

THE GREAT SCOT

Looking back, it seems impossible that anyone other than Sean Connery might have been chosen to bring James Bond to the big screen. He not only had the physicality and sex appeal that one might presuppose of a dashing secret agent, but he had the crucial twinkle in his eye—the knowing good humor—that would set the Bond movies apart, and bulwark the franchise as it endured down the decades. Connery was, like Bond himself, the perfect man for this assignment.

But in fact the actor, barely in his thirties, wasn't well known in the early 1960s, and wasn't on Ian Fleming's short list, once the producers Cubby Broccoli and Harry Saltzman were moving in earnest to make a movie out of the Bond novel *Dr. No.* The author's choice would have been debonair David Niven, whom he admired greatly, followed as a possibility by Cary Grant, Richard Burton or Jimmy Stewart. Those last two nominees—Welsh and American—prove that there was no entry-level criteria that Bond had to be played by an Englishman. This would prove a good thing because Sir Thomas Sean Connery has always felt stridently, "I am not an Englishman, I was never an Englishman, and I don't ever want to be one. I am a Scotsman!"

Indeed. He was born on August 25, 1930, in Edinburgh to a father who worked in a factory and drove a lorry and a mother who toiled as a cleaning woman. On his paternal side there was a certain amount of Irish blood, but the rest was Scottish—his maternal grandparents spoke Scots Gaelic—and Sean (the name he preferred, though he was also called Tommy in his boyhood) was bloody proud of the fact. When he joined the Royal Navy he assumed two tattoos that he still wears today. "Mum and Dad" reads one, and the other: "Scotland Forever."

After his discharge, Connery worked alternately as a milkman, a truck driver (like his father), a lifeguard at the public baths, a laborer on construction projects, a coffin polisher and, in the one job that doesn't fit that pattern, an artist's model at the Edinburgh College of Art, this last at 15 shillings per hour. Or maybe it does fit the pattern. He had sprouted as a lad, reached his adult height of six-foot-two by 18 and was an inarguably impressive physical specimen. So this, too—

the modeling gig—was all about strength and musculature, as was the construction work. It had been suggested to Connery by Archie Brennan, a former Mr. Scotland; one of the students at the art school later remembered young Connery's form as "too beautiful for words, a virtual Adonis." There is some question as to whether Connery placed third in the 1950 Mr. Universe contest, as he has claimed, or whether

MIRRORPIX/EVERETT

OPPOSITE: The aspirant actor in 1957. Above: Fourteen-year-old Sean in his Sea Cadet uniform during World War II. Perhaps the getup was predictive. Connery would go on to enlist in the Royal Navy, and James Bond, his most famous alter ego, who of course had not yet been imagined by Ian Fleming, would have been, in 1944, a commander in Naval Intelligence.

POPPERFOTO/GETTY

he placed at all—then or, maybe, in 1953. Be that as it may, he was certainly in the contest at one point, because a fellow competitor remembered him landing a small part in *South Pacific* during a break in the bodybuilding auditions. In this early stage of his career, looks and physical prowess would carry him.

In the 1950s, Connery landed a host of roles in mostly British films, building to the lead in the 1959 Walt Disney movie *Darby O'Gill and the Little People.* The many of us who have come to know and love all things Sean Connery consider him nothing but charming in *Darby O'Gill.* The *New York Times* critic of the moment, A.H. Weiler, saw him as "merely tall, dark and handsome." Those attributes have, of course, never been disqualifiers in Hollywood, and after he parlayed the twee Disney turn with a success in a 1961 BBC television production of Tolstoy's *Anna Karenina* opposite Claire Bloom, Connery, if not yet a player, was a comer.

He was tapped as Bond. Cubby Broccoli's wife said something along the lines of, "whooo-ahh!" and one of Ian Fleming's lady friends averred, discreetly, that the young Scotsman had a certain je ne sais quoi (even as she knew darned well what the *quoi* was). Fleming remained doubtful: "He's not what I envisioned of James Bond looks. I'm looking for Commander Bond and not an overgrown stunt man." But then the movie opened well, and the writer changed his tune. In fact, in later books,

CONNERY KNEW by 1956 where he hoped to head—the acting life—but he still had to make ends meet, and he had progressed in one of his many jobs, modeling, from posing for art-school students in Edinburgh to featuring clothes in magazine adverts (above). Right: Only a few years later, he was well-known, but still remembered how to strike a pose in a nanosecond when emerging from a Mercedes.

the author gave his man Bond a Swiss-*Scottish* heritage: Fleming's grateful and graceful tribute, Connery's revenge.

Connery had worked with director Terence Young in the 1950s, and if the character of Bond was first molded on the life and personality of Ian Fleming, it took on, cinematically, aspects of Young. "Terence took Sean under his wing," Lois Maxwell, who played Miss Moneypenny in 14 Bond movies, told Connery biographer Robert Cotton. "He took him to dinner, showed him how to walk, how to talk, even how to eat. Some cast members remarked that Connery was simply doing a Terence Young impression." Crucially, Connery and Young shared a sense of humor. James Bond, as written, had none. But Young sensed, correctly, that one of the strengths of *Dr. No* was its relative lightness and ebullience compared with darker spy movies (and to the Bond novels). With the second film, *From Russia with Love*, he continued this gentle turn away from grimness and toward a winking whimsy. It made all the difference.

Connery had been reluctant to commit to a series of films, but did so, and finally made the first five "official" movies (*Dr. No, From Russia with Love, Goldfinger, Thunderball* and *You Only Live Twice*); a sixth after the short-lived George Lazenby experiment (*Diamonds Are Forever*); and a seventh outside the Eon-produced roster (the cheekily titled *Never Say Never Again*). As all of this took more than two decades' time, he of course branched out, coming—gradually—to be regarded as one of the world's finest actors and true superstars. "If America had been discovered as many times as I have," he once said wanly, "no one would remember Columbus." He starred in *Marnie, Indiana Jones and the Last Crusade, The Hunt for Red October,* the forgotten gem *Robin and Marian* (opposite Audrey Hepburn), *The Man Who Would Be King* and *Dragonheart*, and won his Oscar for Best Supporting Actor in 1988 for *The Untouchables.* The following year, age 59, he was named *People* magazine's Sexiest Man Alive ("well, there aren't very many sexy dead men, are there?" he commented self-deprecatingly), and a decade after that he was voted Sexiest Man of the Century. He also won balloting as the Greatest Living Scot, and was knighted Sir Thomas Sean—wearing full Highland dress, by Queen Elizabeth II, in Edinburgh's Holyrood Palace, two years after reportedly having been passed over for his fierce Scottish nationalism—in July of 2000.

It is safe to say much of this would not have happened without James Bond. But Connery has warred with the spy his entire career. "I care about Bond and what happens to him," he said once. "You cannot be connected with a character for this long and not have an interest." But at other instances he has claimed that he wished Bond would just go away. He has never had that wish fulfilled, and that's a good thing. For him, and for us all.

EVERETT

ON CUE IN 1962, Connery became Bond and the press clamored for the at-home story. Later that year, following the filming of *Dr. No,* the actor plays billiards in his basement flat in London (opposite), and at top, during the same shoot, he heads off for a game of golf. Above: It is December 1964, and Connery, now a megastar after the release of *Goldfinger,* is on the set with his wife, the Australian actress Diane Cilento (who had been nominated for a Best Supporting Actress Oscar for 1963's *Tom Jones*). In *You Only Live Twice,* she was the stunt swimming double for Connery's costar Mie Hama in a diving scene. The couple would divorce in 1973.

ODD MAN N

The membership of this actor in the Bond brotherhood is the ultimate curiosity. Here is (or *was*; Niven died in 1983) the actor who was Ian Fleming's first choice for the role. Here is a World War II veteran who seemed the walking embodiment of Bond as written. And here is a big British movie star who finally got to play the role—but as satire. Goofy satire, at that.

This seems almost unfair, for David Niven was as tied to Bond, via Fleming—and as perfect for one particular vision of Bond, if not the super-successful Connery vision—as any actor of the 1950s and '60s. It has been rumored that Fleming wrote *Casino Royale* with Niven in mind. This may well have been so. In the novel, Fleming compares Bond's style and appearance to the devilishly handsome American songwriter and performer Hoagy Carmichael, but certainly something of Niven's insouciance and charisma can be seen in Carmichael. Moreover, Fleming did pay direct tribute to Niven more than once in subsequent episodes of the spy series. In a bit of trivia, Niven is the only actor ever to play Bond who is mentioned by name in the texts—one time each in *On Her Majesty's Secret Service* (in which Bond stays at a luxe Swiss ski resort said to be a favorite of Niven's) and *You Only Live Twice* (in which Niven is called Hollywood's one true gentleman, an opinion with wide concurrence in the film community of the time). As for the novel *Casino Royale* itself, it is known that, as soon as it was published in 1953, Fleming sent a copy in admiration to Niven, and the actor considered adapting it as an episode for the anthology series *Four Star Playhouse*.

Beyond all of Niven's interesting six-degrees connections to James Bond is the man himself—certainly, with Sean Connery, one of the two most distinguished actors to ever assay the role (and the only other Oscar winner).

James David Graham Niven was born in London on March 1, 1910, into a family of some social standing; his biological father was probably his mother's lover rather than her husband, but interestingly, considering Connery's heritage and that of the fictive

Bond, Niven was very proud of his legal father's Scottish lineage and often claimed to have been born in Scotland. Prone to misbehavior at school, he straightened out at the Royal Military College at Sandhurst and rose to the rank of second lieutenant in the Highland Light Infantry. He meanwhile left the military and traveled to America, living first in New York and then Los Angeles, where he caught the acting bug. By the 1930s, he was landing small roles. When Britain declared war on Germany in World War II in 1939,

NIVEN'S FIRST WIFE, Primmie, was tragically killed in an accidental fall at actor Tyrone Power's house shortly after the family relocated to the U.S. in 1946; she was only 28. Above are her and David's two children, Jamie and David Jr., with their stepmother, the former fashion model Hjördis, shortly after her marriage to Niven in 1948. Due in no small part to Hjördis's alcoholism, her and David's marriage would not be an easy one, but would endure until his death. Opposite: Niven and Best Actress Award winner Susan Hayward with their Oscars in 1959.

Niven returned home, resumed his lieutenant's role and transferred to the storied Commandos unit. He went on to perform nobly in combat during the Allies' final push toward Germany. He later told humorous stories about his war experiences—"Look, you chaps only have to do this once," he said to his men before they leapt into battle, "but I'll have to do it all over again in Hollywood with Errol Flynn!"—though he was reluctant to glorify his service. Winston Churchill was not so reticent, however, upon meeting Niven during the war: "Young man, you did a very fine thing to give up a most promising career to fight for your country. Mark you, had you not done so—it would have been despicable."

Needless to say, the film career was not sacrificed, and Niven returned to the screen newly popular with the masses. He is perhaps best remembered for *The Bishop's Wife* (1947), *Around the World in 80 Days* (1956), *Separate Tables* (for which he won the 1958 Academy Award for Best Actor), and certainly for his portrayal of Sir Charles Lytton, the suave jewel thief known as the Phantom, in *The Pink Panther* (1963). He is also remembered, always with a smile, by Bond fans. They are quick to point out that of the six male and female James or Jimmy Bonds who adopted the name at one point or another in the chaotic 1967 *Casino Royale*—a menagerie of ersatz spies hoping to confuse and otherwise bedevil SMERSH—Niven's character was supposed to be the real one. Sort of.

If the Broccolis, who have done anything but encourage interloping films while they have worked their way through the Bond library, were not amused, it can be assumed that Ian Fleming, had he still been alive, might have been. He had wanted Niven to play Bond. Finally, the odd man in, Niven did so.

Niven, then 73, passed away in 1983 in Chateau-d'Oex, Switzerland, the country that supplied the second half of James Bond's made-up heritage and boasted, high in its Alps, a ski getaway that was once a favorite of . . .

Well, not only of Bond but also of Hollywood star David Niven.

HERE WE HAVE two of the greats of postwar British cinema, Peter Sellers and David Niven, in the original *Pink Panther* film in 1963. (The movie's tagline: "You only live once . . . so see *The Pink Panther* twice!") Needless to say, Sellers's Inspector Clouseau was a defining role, and Niven would return to his part as Sir Charles Litton—the Phantom—in cameo bits in much later *Pink Panther* films. He was sick with Lou Gehrig's disease by then, and his voice was dubbed by impressionist Rich Little, but he had remained friends with the director Blake Edwards through the years, and it was just the kind of thing Niven would do. He and Sellers would of course reunite in the satiric Bond caper of 1967, *Casino Royale*.

EVERETT

IN SEARCH OF THE NEXT BOND

Sean Connery was ready to walk—he had said as much, and *Time* magazine, for one, thought that maybe he would. "Connery seems uncomfortable and fatigued, as if he meant it when he said that this would be his last Bond film," *Time* opined in its June 30, 1967, review of *You Only Live Twice*. "It may just be an off year for 007; it may be that he has received too much ribbing from [the satiric film] *Casino Royale*. But it could also be that the monumental Bond issue is at long last beginning to deflate."

Time was right about one thing, dead wrong about another. Connery was indeed done—for a while. Money would entice him to make *Diamonds Are Forever* and *Never Say Never Again* further on down the road. But here we are 45 years later—not the "at long last" five years that was *Time*'s vantage in '67—and the Bond issue is inflating once more, big time, with *Skyfall*. Economists might disagree, but it seems some bubbles never burst.

The Bond series has survived Connery's long-ago malaise, and it has survived Eon Productions' bizarre decision to solve its sudden, post-Connery personnel problem with a casting call. Yes, of course there was scuttlebutt about landing a name actor—Clint Eastwood, fresh off his success as The Man With No Name? Roger Moore, the debonair TV star of *The Saint*? But finally it was: "Come one, come all, ye Bonds out there! Step right up! Who wants to be the next James Bond?!"

Four hundred actors did, which seems odd only because the number wasn't 4 million. Producers Cubby Broccoli and Harry Saltzman, along with Peter R. Hunt, the director of the next planned film, *On Her Majesty's Secret Service*, whittled the candidates to five. (One actor considered was a young Timothy Dalton, whom Broccoli would remember.) Then they did what big-budget movie productions did back in 1967: They called LIFE magazine, and asked if we wanted a peek at the final auditions. We said sure, and sent staff photographer Loomis Dean to London, where Hunt was putting the five and a number of aspiring Bond girls through their paces.

Most all of the photographs shown here did not appear in the original magazine article, and several are far more amusing than the ones that did run. The picture on the opposite page is a composite assembled in LIFE's offices, and the original caption on page 121 of the October 11, 1968, issue read: "'An instant millionaire'—that is what producers Broccoli and Saltzman say the new Bond will be. Finalists in the competition are (from left) John Richardson, Hans De Vries, Robert Campbell, Anthony Rogers and George Lazenby. Averaging in height 6 feet 2 inches and in age 32, all speak with a neat British accent." That took some acting by Lazenby, an Aussie, who is also seen in the photograph on this page relaxing with fellow Bond-mates between sessions. Ultimately, the competition came down to him and Richardson, who perhaps had the inside track, having costarred with Raquel Welch in the bizarre but bona fide box office hit of 1966, *One Million Years B.C.* (Richardson did not wear the fur bikini.) On the pages immediately following: Campbell primps and then secures a prop, his Q-issued shoulder holster. Lazenby loosens up, good-naturedly, during the tense auditions.

NO DOUBT it was hard work under a lot of pressure, but somebody had to do it. In the photo at right, top, before a take, a cameraman measures distance for John Richardson, as director Peter R. Hunt seems to be praying that something might work out. His was an understandable posture: Hunt had served as film editor and/or second unit director on earlier films in the Bond series and was finally getting his big shot with *On Her Majesty's Secret Service*. As fate would have it, this would be his as well as George Lazenby's first and last James Bond picture in the principal roles of director and star. (Hunt later lamented that he felt Lazenby could have been the best-ever Bond if he had continued in the part.) Certainly these photographs indicate that Hunt well understood how important the delicate male–female relationship was to the Bond story. At right, bottom, he counsels Richardson to proceed just so, and on the opposite page, top row, Richardson gives it his best shot (which would prove only second-best, perhaps thanks to Hunt's no doubt distracting gaze). In the middle row, Robert Campbell (left) and Anthony Rogers make their moves. In the bottom row, one of the Bond Girl hopefuls repairs any damage done before the next round, and Lazenby is, well, in like Flynn and has won the role. All will be nothing but roses from here on, right?

LOOMIS DEAN (8)

THE UNLUCKY WINNER

No question. There was something about George Lazenby that set him apart from the four other Bond hopefuls we have just met. The usual argument—the studio's *mea explicatione,* if you will—is that it was his extraordinary good looks, which had, after all, made him the highest paid male model in Europe at the time. Anyone could have made the mistake! Some may say it was his ample confidence and arrogance. "I've even done things Bond never did," he told LIFE back when, "things you couldn't print."

Yes . . . well . . .

Surely it wasn't his résumé: He had nary an acting gig to his name at the time, save for a few commercials. But in any event, during those auditions Lazenby had impressed the uppers with his looks, his cocksurety and his martial arts expertise, breaking the nose of a stuntman during a staged knife fight. He also amused them by having spent months of posturing as the world's favorite (and now most famous) spy. Hearing that the role was up for grabs, Lazenby had begun preparing: purchasing a suit from Sean Connery's Savile Row tailor and a fancy Bond-esque Rolex watch. He was seen around town in a Jaguar, and—get this! Bond himself was never so brazen!—he began having his locks trimmed by Cubby Broccoli's barber. It was at the barbershop, in fact, where Lazenby first, shall we say, bumped into Broccoli, who was struck by the young man's resemblance to the imagined Bond and made a mental note of him as a future candidate for the role.

So let us deduce the 29-year-old Lazenby beat out the other spy-worthy men because of all these singularities and happenstances and strategies. It's unimportant now. What was important at the time: Would Lazenby's turn as Bond in the sixth installment of the series, *On Her Majesty's Secret Service,* be the career catapult George was looking for? And would he measure up? Phrased another way: Could he walk a mile in Sean Connery's shoes?

Or was he, as he dove into his future fate, perhaps getting ahead of himself?

"I'm really looking forward to being James Bond for the bread and the birds," he told LIFE upon securing the role. Would Bond have said that's why he entered the spy game? No, he would not have.

Who was and is George Lazenby? A small-town boy born in 1939 in New South Wales, Australia, he studied chemical engineering, did his service in the Australian army and broke sales records as a car salesman. After migrating to swinging London in 1964, he continued to hawk cars, one day making a sale to a photographer who suggested the big, handsome guy try modeling. Lazenby took the man's advice and within a few short years he was a top model, doing television and print ads, even taking a turn as the European Marlboro Man. Before long—certainly, before long enough—he was James Bond. In a 1992 interview, an older and wiser Lazenby, showing none of the bravado on display for LIFE decades earlier, reminisced to *Entertainment Tonight:* "I was so naïve, so green. I was a country boy from Australia, basically, who walked into a Bond role."

Yes, but one of life's cruelties is that a person can only live life at the time in question, not in retrospect. Lazenby was rumored to have been an on-set prima donna, demanding and difficult. The

© 1982 RON AVERY/MPTVIMAGES

IN 1982, Lincoln Continental figured there was enough Lazenby love lingering to cast him in a Bond-flavored commercial (above). Opposite: The new guy in '69.

film got made nevertheless, and whether anyone on the production thought Lazenby was any good—he wasn't, as nearly a half century of George Lazenby jokes have certified—the movie itself was fine, and on the eve of its premiere, Lazenby looked like the future. Then, just before the film opened, he shocked Bond film execs by proclaiming on national television he would not be returning as 007. Not even a seven-picture deal worth a reported $28 million (what were they thinking?!?) could change his tune. Apparently Lazenby thought (or was advised) that the arising hippie culture would render the franchise passé, and that offers for bigger roles would pour in. Hubris, thou art a cruel mistress.

After his single turn as James Bond, Lazenby did little for a while, then in 1973 he was set to star alongside Bruce Lee in a film slated to be the biggest-budgeted martial arts film to that date. This film would have marked George's big post-Bond comeback. Unfortunately, Lee passed away suddenly before filming began. Fate was not fair to Lazenby's movie career, beginning with his passing the audition.

Still, he has had a steady stream of work over the years in television, in films, voice-overs and commercials. Today, Lazenby—73, a father of five (a sixth child has passed away), living in L.A.—is not without regret: "I look back and think, 'How did that happen?' I had no idea where I was going when I got into the Bond film. When I became famous I didn't know how to handle it, so it almost drove me crazy. I'd loved to have had that time over again and done one or two [more Bond movies], it would have worked out

DOSSIER

NATIONALITY: Australian

BOND MOVIES: 1

AGE WHEN HE WAS BOND: 30

HAIR: Dark brown

EYES: Brown

HEIGHT: 6'2"

PRIOR DISTINCTIONS: Big Fry Guy for Fry's Chocolate; European Marlboro Man

QUOTE: "I look at Bond films only if I have to. I've got some sad memories."

APPALOOSA PICTURES/IONIAN/RONALD GRANT ARCHIVE/MARY EVANS

great for me." Though the passage of time has been kind to *On Her Majesty's Secret Service* as a whole (*Entertainment Weekly* ranked the film the sixth-best Bond), George Lazenby is remembered, by those who remember, as the youngest Bond; the most surprising Bond; and the guy who played the role just once—and then handed in his gun.

GEORGE PLACES the wrong bet. At left we see what might have happened to James Bond if he had opted for the early retirement he contemplated in the novel *Casino Royale*; this is Lazenby only one year on from his most famous role. Above, another year further on, in 1971, he appears in a much-more-relevant-than-Bond film, *Universal Soldier.* Right: Guesting with Victoria Principal and series star Jack Lord in a 1979 episode of *Hawaii Five-O.* Perhaps Lord empathized: He himself had been an excellent Felix Leiter in *Dr. No* but never reprised the role. Reports differ as to why: Either Lord asked for a big raise and costar billing with Connery, and Broccoli balked, or Broccoli feared Lord's Leiter could overshadow Connery's Bond.

JAMES GRAY/DAILY MAIL/REX USA

EVERETT

INTERCESSIONS OF A SAINT

After Lazenby's hasty departure, producers Broccoli and Saltzman found themselves scrambling just as they had when Sean Connery announced what would be the first of his three retirements as Bond. They behaved as before, holding auditions for the seventh installment of the franchise, *Diamonds Are Forever*. But they were ultimately persuaded by United Artists to return to Connery and ask if he would return to the role. Connery was convinced by an added number of zeros, and agreed to take what he earnestly felt would be his final spin as 007. (A quick aside here: It has long been about the money for Connery, and for the Broccolis. The young actor was paid approximately $100,000 for *Dr. No,* and that figure grew to $1 million by the time he first left the team. He accepted $1,250,000 [which he gave to his Scottish education foundation] plus a percentage [which amounted to $6 million] for *Diamonds Are Forever,* and then earned $5 million when he engineered the renegade 1983 production, *Never Say Never Again.* In the Daniel Craig era, he has said from the sidelines that he would consider returning to the Bond films as a villain—that sure would be fun!—but doubted that the Broccolis would pay him what he's worth. There have been no reports of negotiations.)

So Connery made *Diamonds Are Forever,* and then the 007 job opening was posted anew. The good news was, there was another

EVERETT

KEYSTONE/GETTY

popular British secret agent operating in the filmic shadows, and at this point he stepped forth and made himself available for a new assignment. Enter, bow tie, dinner jacket and handgun at the ready, Roger Moore.

Born in Stockwell, London, in October 1927, Moore had a relatively ordinary childhood: his father was a policeman, Roger attended school, did a brief stint at university, and fulfilled his duties in the National Service. Just by the way: At the Royal Academy of Dramatic Arts, where he studied acting in the mid-1940s, Moore met Canadian contemporary Lois Maxwell, who would also find Bond fame as the original (and 14-time) Miss Moneypenny.

Moore, still a teenager, got his professional start doing bit parts in British movies including the "box office stinker" *Caesar and Cleopatra,* starring Vivien Leigh and Claude Rains, and then began to appear on television. In 1953 he made the leap across the pond, where his good

ENGLISH THROUGH and through and somewhere between a hunk and a pretty boy in the 1950s (left), Roger Moore was always a possibility as Bond. Moreover, everyone liked him and was happy to work with him. Producer Cubby Broccoli, who had often been at swords' points with Sean Connery, could play cards or backgammon on the set with Moore, and both men were happy to engage. Opposite: In 1968, the "Saint" seems to be auditioning for less saintly stuff with cigarettes and martinis.

PETER RUCK/BIPS/GETTY

DOSSIER

NATIONALITY: English

BOND MOVIES: 7

AGE WHEN HE WAS BOND: 45–57

HAIR: Blond/light brown (hair dyed darker in all of his Bond movies)

EYES: Blue

HEIGHT: 6'1"

PRIOR DISTINCTIONS: The embodiment of Simon Templar

QUOTE: "Today, I am completely opposed to small arms and what they can do to children. I played every role tongue in cheek because I don't really believe in that sort of hero. I don't like guns."

looks and talent were noticed by MGM. The studio offered Moore a contract in 1954, and as a hired hand he appeared in films such as *The Last Time I Saw Paris.* After turns as a series regular on the television shows *Maverick, Ivanhoe* and *The Alaskans,* Moore finally got his big break. In 1962 he was cast as Simon Templar in the British television series *The Saint.*

Based on the well-known Leslie Charteris stories, which recount the vigilante adventures of Templar, *The Saint* evolved throughout the 1960s—no doubt, because of the influence of the popular Bond movies—from a series of straight mysteries to secret agent thrillers. The show, an immediate success in Great Britain, was eventually distributed internationally, including in America. Moore's fame went from regional to worldwide, and not only was he inextricably associated with the character, he ultimately became co-owner of the franchise. When he might have raised his hand for Bond, he couldn't.

When the seven-year run of *The Saint* finally ended in 1969, Moore returned to the big screen in forgettable films such as *The Man Who Haunted Himself.* He could not shake his gentleman-detective-cum-spy persona, so perhaps it was no surprise to anyone except maybe Moore himself, who figured he was too old for the role, when the Bond folks came calling.

Although Moore was 45 when he began *Live and Let Die,* his age proved no deterrent, and he would go on to appear as Bond six more times. He is remembered today as the humorous and witty version. Moore once explained his approach to the part thusly: "To me, the Bond situations are so ridiculous . . . I mean, this man is supposed to be a spy and yet, everybody knows he's a spy. Every bartender in the world offers him martinis that are shaken, not stirred. It's outrageous. So you have to treat the humor outrageously as well."

By the time Moore took his seventh Bond spin in *A View to a Kill,* his age was clearly showing, and in 1985, at 58, he announced he was retiring, claiming he was embarrassed to do love scenes with women who were the same age as his daughter. He remains the oldest-ever 007 and is tied with Connery at seven portrayals.

After bidding adieu to Bond's boats, cars and women, Moore found himself with a lesser career in movies and TV. He began to look elsewhere. In August of 1991, he

followed friend Audrey Hepburn's lead as a Goodwill Ambassador for UNICEF, for which he subsequently raised millions of dollars. In recognition of his good works, Moore was made a Commander of the Order of the British Empire in 1999 and was knighted in 2003.

As opposed to Sir Sean, Sir Roger has embraced his Bondness. He became a keen mate of Cubby Broccoli's (he attended the funeral in 1996; Connery did not), and wrote a memoir entitled *My Word Is My Bond.* Now nearly 85, Sir Roger continues with his humanitarian work, has contributed a foreword to another Bond retrospective book in this golden anniversary year and good-naturedly introduces himself to strangers as, "Moore . . . Roger Moore."

WHEN YOUNG, there was no question that Moore was handsome and sexy (above, in 1957, with then wife Dorothy Squires). Later, as Bond, there was always a question about whether he was still young enough, and Moore always did his darndest to make the case (left, in Jamaica, in 1972, just as he was accepting the role).

JOHN PRATT/KEYSTONE/GETTY

DAVID STEEN/CAMERA PRESS/REDUX

DOSSIER

NATIONALITY: Welsh

BOND MOVIES: 2

AGE WHEN HE WAS BOND: 43–45

HAIR: Dark brown

EYES: Gray-green

HEIGHT: 6'2"

PRIOR DISTINCTIONS: Success in the West End and in *Masterpiece Theatre*–type films and TV miniseries

QUOTE: "You can't relate to a superhero, to a superman, but you can identify with a real man who in times of crisis draws forth some extraordinary quality from within himself and triumphs but only after a struggle. Real courage is knowing what faces you and knowing how to face it."

MAN OF DUTY

When Roger Moore relinquished the Bond reins in 1985, there was in some quarters hot and heavy (shall we say) speculation (and desire) that the über-handsome Pierce Brosnan would take his place. However, Brosnan, as had once been the case with Moore, had prior commitments—in his case a contract with Mary Tyler Moore Productions to continue as TV's *Remington Steele*. And so, who? The bar literally had been set at a certain height. When five-foot-nine movie star Mel Gibson once had expressed an interest in being Bond, United Artists had been keen but Cubby Broccoli had nixed the thought, insisting that Bond was and must always be tall. Timothy Dalton was six-foot-two, and therefore he was in the game. When, in 1986, Broccoli attended a West End production of *The Taming of the Shrew* the actor was starring in, Dalton reintroduced himself to the producer nearly 20 years after first discussing the possibility of replacing Connery. Seeing Dalton onstage, Broccoli took note. He always registered an interesting face (and height), and he always did his homework.

What he learned about Dalton was that the actor had studied at the Royal Academy of Dramatic Art for two years in the mid-1960s. In the '70s, he was involved with the august Royal Shakespeare Company, and was featured in productions of *Romeo and Juliet* and *Love's Labour's Lost*, among other plays. His screen appearances piled up in historical dramas—Lord Darnley in *Mary, Queen of Scots*, Dr. Thomas Rock in *The Doctor and the Devils*—and his reputation grew, in recognition of his range and talent.

Dalton's portrayal of James Bond, especially before Daniel Craig took on the role, was routinely referred to as the "literary" or "Ian Fleming" interpretation. His Bond had none of the campy humor of Roger Moore's Bond, and was less reliant on Q-type mechanical gimmickry. He was a dark killer who didn't even seem to have time to jump from bed to bed. In tune with the AIDS-fearing times, Dalton's was a one-woman (per movie) Bond.

This sea change got mixed reviews. *The New York Times* saw Dalton as "perfectly at home as an angry Bond, and as a romantic lead and as an action hero." But *Entertainment Weekly* called Dalton names: "Bland . . . James Bland." The magazine bothered to add that Dalton's politically correct monogamy was a low point in the history of the Bond franchise.

The only voice that mattered was, of course, vox populi, and the audience voted a mild thumbs-down at the box office to *The Living Daylights* in 1987 and *Licence to Kill* in 1989.

Post-Bond, Dalton has kept himself busy enough, recently providing the voice of Mr. Pricklepants in the 2010 hit *Toy Story 3* and playing Chief Inspector Jones in the acclaimed film *The Tourist*. As for the franchise: If he left it briefly shaken, stirred and even, the less kind might say, on the rocks, it was right and ready for a revival.

SEVERAL HOITY-TOITY CRITICS thought—and still think—that Dalton was the best actor to ever take on the Bond role. They made arguments on his behalf that the spy nonsense was simply beneath him. What they liked, by contrast, was *Le Voyeur*, opposite, a 1970 film in which Dalton plays opposite legends Virni Lisi and Marcello Mastroianni, or 1971's *Mary, Queen of Scots*, above, which stars, in the title role, none other than Vanessa Redgrave, with whom he had a stormy 15-year-long relationship.

MAN OF STEELE

You could say that Pierce Brosnan, like Sean Connery, got to play James Bond and get away with it. This is to say: He took on a role that was designed to typecast its player, went along with the typecasting, then emerged from BondWorld and, with deft decision-making and fine performances, reinvented himself as an actor. "When you play a role like that you live with it forever," the always agreeable and clear-eyed Brosnan has said, implying that he's happy enough to accept this salient fact. He just doesn't want 007 to define him.

It never could have been predicted that young Pierce, who was born to poor circumstances and a quickly broken home in rural Ireland, would one day make his greatest fame as a slick, wise-cracking, gun-toting playboy spy in flawless Brioni suits. His mother was still in her teens when she gave birth in 1953, and Pierce's father had walked out before his son was a year old. Desperate, his mother, whom Pierce credits deeply, went to London to pursue nursing. She remarried and was finally able to bring her boy across. In England, young Brosnan felt like an outsider; his nickname in school was "Irish." But he now had his eyes opened to a wider world. Among the things he was impressed by were movies—and, in fact, Bond. Like many 10- or 11-year-old boys of the time, his first experience with the secret agent was through the larger-than-life hit *Goldfinger.* "I remember the girl, the lovely gold girl," Brosnan reminisced later of the day his stepfather took him to the movie house. "I was a country boy, green as grass, and there was this naked gold lady. It was very moving to various parts of my young psyche." Well, yes.

At 16, he decided traditional academics were not for him and quit school to become a commercial artist; Brosnan still paints, and paints very well. He also had an affinity for acting, which delivered him to the acclaimed Drama Centre in London, where he studied under the dancer and acting teacher, Yat Malmgren, who had also tutored Sean Connery, among many others. A more consequential bridge to Bond was built when Brosnan's first wife, the Australian actress Cassandra Harris (who would die after an illness in 1991), was cast in a Bond film, and on the set Brosnan was introduced to

COURTESY PIERCE BROSNAN

BEGORRA, he was a good-looking young laddie! Above is the Irish boy in his Sunday best, and opposite is Brosnan in 1986, just as he is about to leave his TV cross behind and realize—at last—what it is like to be the planet's reigning James Bond. Two aspects beyond argument: He's tall enough and handsome enough. Also, he has that slender "comma" of hair falling on his forehead that Ian Fleming described in the books.

CAMERA PRESS/REDUX

DOSSIER

NATIONALITY: Irish

BOND MOVIES: 4

AGE WHEN HE WAS BOND: 42–49

HAIR: Brown

EYES: Blue

HEIGHT: 6'1$^1/_2$"

PRIOR DISTINCTIONS: The name was Steele . . . Remington Steele.

QUOTE: "It never felt real to me. I never felt I had complete ownership over Bond. Because you'd always have to do these stupid one-liners—which I loathed—and I always felt phony doing them."

the big man himself: Cubby Broccoli, who would remember him.

Blessed with carefree handsomeness, he found roles in television, and a fateful audition led to his ticket stateside to play a criminal turned private investigator in the series *Remington Steele*. For five years Brosnan chased bad guys and looked for all the world like a small-screen Sean Connery of the early Bond years. Cubby was

hardly alone in seeing an heir apparent in the right-size, right-age Irishman. When NBC decided to cancel *Steele* due to low ratings, it appeared Brosnan would be free of his seven-year contract and able to follow graybeard Roger Moore as the next James Bond. Brosnan had already popped a bottle of champagne to celebrate—he literally had—when all of the publicity that his career move had generated convinced NBC to give *Steele* a further shot. Brosnan was out and Dalton was in for the 1987 edition, *The Living Daylights. Steele* did end not long after, but the Bond franchise would soon be on an induced hiatus, tied up in the courts for a goodly while. This may have turned out to be a good thing, for Brosnan appeared in the interim in several movies, including *Mrs. Doubtfire*, establishing his own film persona before accepting his initial assignment from M.

His four Bond movies, released from 1995 to 2002, were solidly successful at the box office and put the secret agent back on his feet. As for the star's turn in the lead role, it was, thanks to his rakish gorgeousness, simply too easy to have sport with, and the critics were measured as they watched him progress from *GoldenEye* ("he makes a fabulous clothing model") through *Tomorrow Never Dies* ("its hero is chronically overdressed") and *The World Is Not Enough* ("Pierce Brosnan bears noticeably more resemblance to a real human being") to *Die Another Day* ("This Bond is curiously vulnerable, decidedly flappable underneath the cynical urbanity"). Well, at least they saw something.

There were plans for a fifth Brosnan film, but things got complicated. Brosnan says that over too many apple martinis, he and filmmaker Quentin Tarantino hatched a plan to make *Casino Royale* together. That might have been wild, but the Bond producers said no. Then they bid Brosnan adieu after the kind of rampant speculation that attended his entrance, and Daniel Craig was signed. Brosnan hasn't yet seen the recent movies, though he tried to, once, on an airplane: "I figured 37,000 feet was a good distance to watch it from, but then the machine broke on me—twice. I thought, [Expletive] it. He's the man now. He owns it. And fair play to him."

As it turned out, Brosnan didn't need the gig. Embarking smartly on an "anti-Bond period," he drew acclaim as a foul-mouthed hit man in *The Matador* (2005) and charmed the women in a new way with a bit of singing and free-spirited acting opposite Meryl Streep and alongside Colin Firth in *Mamma Mia!* (2008). He was praised as well for *The Ghost Writer* (2010). Personally, he found his causes in charitable work and environmental activism, and married the American journalist Keely Shaye Smith in 2001. He became a United States citizen in 2004.

His story recounts a long journey from west-of-nowhere Ireland, with the James Bond experience seeming like one exciting chapter.

FAMILY MAN. Brosnan, wife Cassie Harris and son Sean share a bath in their Hollywood Hills home (opposite), and (right) Brosnan, Harris and her two children from a previous marriage, Christopher and Charlotte, wonder, "Who's there?" Brosnan's marriage profile is like Niven's: a first wife who died tragically young (Cassie at 43 of ovarian cancer in 1991), then a second long-lasting union.

DOSSIER

NATIONALITY: English

BOND MOVIES: 3

AGE WHEN HE WAS BOND: 38–44

HAIR: Blond, steadfastly blond

EYES: Blue

HEIGHT: 5'10" (He has worn lifts while playing Bond.)

PRIOR DISTINCTIONS: Art-house hero, but able to acquit himself in an Angelina Jolie vehicle.

QUOTE: "The simple fact is, the character was pretty much fully formed from the start. Sean Connery nailed it from the beginning. Bond's single-mindedness. His toughness. His ruthlessness. He wasn't infallible, but he always knew the answer, always knew exactly what to do in any situation. And he always knew how to wear a suit."

BOND REBOOTED

H e knew he had a shot and then he knew he had the inside track. He spent several excruciating days and booze-filled nights trying to figure it all out, asking friends and confidants—and himself—whether or not he should become the next James Bond. Some pals said, "You've got to do it." Others tried to talk him out of it. In the end, as we know, Daniel Craig took the plunge. He figured it was as much on his own terms as possible: He was to be a *new* Bond, an intelligent action hero in a gritty, dangerous landscape, a Dalton 2.0-plus. In the first of his films, *Casino Royale*, a bartender would ask our simmering antihero if he prefers his martini shaken or stirred. Craig's Bond sneers, "Do I look like I give a damn?" A whole new Bond.

It would be on his terms, but also *theirs*. This was a postmodern multibillion-dollar film franchise (depending on how you measured it, total number of profitable films or total grosses overall, it was right up there with *Harry Potter* and *Lord of the Rings* as one of the most popular—and valuable—movie series ever) and so there were consequences and responsibilities to be acknowledged by all parties. Craig did acknowledge them: "When I accepted the job to work on Bond, I genuinely did it to change my life. I knew that it would flip everything on its head."

It did that—for Daniel Craig, for Commander Bond, and for all of us who were fans of either.

Implicit in his comment: Before Daniel Wroughton Craig received his MI6 license, he was little known to the world audience. A Liverpool lad with a merchant seaman–turned-pub-owner dad and an art teacher mum who took him and his sisters to local plays, Craig dropped out of high school at the precise age Pierce Brosnan had—16—and enrolled at the Guildhall School of Music & Drama at London's Barbican Centre. "I kind of fell in love with the idea of

CRAIG, seen on the opposite page in a 1999 portrait, is the Bond for a new generation in fact as well as in fancy: He is the first of the actors to have been born after the feature-film series began in 1962, and the first to have been born after the 1964 death of Ian Fleming.

acting," he later said. "I liked the idea of it—you know, shouting a lot and dressing up and all that." Speaking of costume (and what his big role did for his career): A 2012 "Fifty Years of Bond Style" exhibition at the esteemed Barbican featured among other items the swim trunks worn by Craig in *Casino Royale*.

An apprenticeship was required before he would wear those trunks and wield a Walther. Craig received good notices as the painter Francis Bacon's lover in the 1998 film *Love Is the Devil*, and nods for supporting roles in Hollywood movies including *Lara Croft: Tomb Raider* (2001) and *Road to Perdition* (2002). Then came *Sylvia* (2003), *Layer Cake* (2004) and *Munich* (2005), with Craig shape-shifting from poet to cocaine dealer to assassin.

Cubby Broccoli had passed away a year after *GoldenEye* was released in 1995, and Craig's would be the first anointment in the "official" series made without his sprinkling of holy water. The actor was only 5 foot 10, which a generation earlier might have disqualified him right there, and he was not only blond but possessed of the notion that he would stay blond during filming. Cubby spun and spun in his grave, but the Broccoli heirs, who were bothering to barter for the rights to the very first novel, which had been beyond the family's grasp for a half century, were firmly focused on the idea that this was, to use the Hollywood term, a "reboot": a reinvention and reinvigoration. Certainly the fresh-blood strategy had been discussed with Craig, who had radical—*dangerous*—ideas of his own: "Bond is supposedly the most-male moment, but to me he's never been macho." *Hmmm.*

Of course there was a backlash. After Craig was cast in *Casino Royale*, websites with names such as danielcraigisnotbond.com were born in protest. Honor Blackman, who had famously played Pussy Galore in *Goldfinger*, bothered to weigh in: "It isn't the character that Ian [Fleming] wrote about. It's not Bond is all I can say." After the film opened, Craig's hair color and inability to smile suavely became rallying points for boo-bird critics and audience members: *He looks like Vladimir Putin!*

The director of *Casino Royale*, Martin Campbell, had directed

GoldenEye, with Pierce Brosnan, and he had a different take: "I think with the gadgets, the invincible car, the huge sort of ice palaces . . . I just thought it got preposterous . . . This time we definitely wanted to go back to a more realistic Bond . . . I think it's in *Casino Royale* where Fleming always said he [Bond] looked like Hoagy Carmichael . . . [Craig] is a very interesting-looking guy and I think he has all the attributes to make a much grittier and tougher Bond."

The defensive posture was unnecessary. Both *Casino Royale* and 2008's *Quantum of Solace* were solid successes worldwide, and Craig's initial Bond outing was the first ever nominated for British Academy Awards for best performance and film. He meanwhile married the actress Rachel Weisz, and continued with his rebooted Daniel Craig career—big stuff (*The Girl with the Dragon Tattoo;* the newest Bond, *Skyfall*) and small (the independent *Flashbacks of a Fool*, done as a favor for a friend). Also, of course, as Bond he was on a not-so-secret assignment on the evening of July 27, 2012, parachuting with Queen Elizabeth II into the Olympic Stadium in London to open the games of the 30th Olympiad.

IN 1998, Craig portrays George Dyer in *Love Is the Devil: Study for a Portrait of Francis Bacon.* His acting chops have never been in question, and in fact four past Bonds—Connery, Moore, Dalton and Brosnan—are on the record that Craig is a good choice for the role. One aspect of Craig that he has had to work at is the glad-handing. He is not comfortable with the red-carpet scene, but some functions are attendance-mandatory in the big-bucks Bond universe. Above: On November 14, 2006, at the Royal Premiere of *Casino Royale* at London's Odeon Leicester Square, Craig shakes the hand of his boss, Her Majesty, whom he will serve dutifully at the Olympics Opening Ceremonies.

IMPOSTORS

Some were blatantly Bond wannabes, some owed a small debt to Bond, some—it could be argued—were even better than Bond. They all rode the wave, when the wave was tidal.

The 1960s: That sure was one topsy-turvy time. It was cool to dress and wear your hair like James Bond, and simultaneously cool to dress and wear your hair like the Beatles. Martinis had a new vogue, while marijuana became a different drug of choice. The Beatles, in *Help!*, satirized James Bond movies.

Which side were you on? Some people—many people—were on both.

We pick Noel Harrison to point up the absurdity of it all. Born in 1934, famously the son of Rex Harrison, he was a two-time Olympic skier for Great Britain in the 1950s. Meantime, he had learned to play the guitar, and in the Swingin' '60s had a first minor hit in the U.S. with "A Young Girl," written by the French mainstream cabaret star Charles Aznavour, and a second with "Suzanne," written by the brooding-poet Canadian Leonard Cohen. Harrison's biggest song back in England was "The Windmills of Your Mind," which was used as the theme song of the caper film *The Thomas Crown Affair*. The song won the Oscar for Best Original Song, and Harrison, in 1968, would have sung it on the show, one year after his dad had performed the winning "Talk to the Animals" from *Dr. Doolittle*, but Noel was off on an acting gig. In this other realm, he is best remembered as Stefanie Powers's sidekick in *The Girl from U.N.C.L.E.*, a spin-off series with an Ian Fleming pedigree (as we'll see). By the 1970s Noel Harrison was playing in *My Fair Lady* as Henry Higgins, his father's signature role.

So what was he? Of which generation was he a member? And does it matter?

It does not, not now, not from the vantage of a half century on. What matters, as we look back at all of this product that arose in the wake of the phenomena, is quality: Were they any good? Badfinger, though no Beatles, was a pretty fine band.

And *The Girl from U.N.C.L.E.*, while not *The Man from U.N.C.L.E.*, was a fun show. It's interesting: Fleming, who had sought a bland name for James Bond, came up with the exotic monikers of both Napoleon Solo and his U.N.C.L.E. associate April Dancer when he was involved in the original series in its earliest stages. He was not involved in the fine British offering *Danger Man*, known in the U.S. as *Secret Agent*, but there is cross-pollination here as well: The terrific actor Patrick McGoohan had been seriously considered as Bond for the *Dr. No* movie but had withdrawn his candidacy because, as a Catholic, he found the sex and violence indecent. Also of quality

were the ground-breaking U.S. TV series *I Spy* and, particularly, *The Ipcress File*, which was positioned as an "anti-Bond" spy film upon its release in 1965, and went on to not only launch Michael Caine to stardom but win Britain's top award as Best Picture.

So these were not "Impostors" so much as homages (*U.N.C.L.E.*) or twists on a theme (*Danger Man* and *Ipcress*). Then you had your *Flint* films and your Matt Helms and *Modesty Blaise:* lesser stuff, to be sure. Ah, but it was a large wave indeed that James Bond churned up back in the day, a wave big enough to raise many boats, boats of all sizes and forms—some shipshape, some pretty leaky.

ON THE PREVIOUS PAGES, clockwise from top left, four quality acts: Bill Cosby, the first African American drama-series TV star, in *I Spy*; Patrick McGoohan, who was once considered for Bond in *Dr. No*, in the TV series *Danger Man* (U.S. title: *Secret Agent*); Michael Caine as Harry Palmer, the protagonist of the excellent 1965 film *The Ipcress File* and its sequels; Robert Vaughn as Napoleon Solo in *The Man from U.N.C.L.E.*, in which role he dangles, hands tied, in the photograph on the opposite page, alongside costar David McCallum, playing Illya Kuryakin. Above: Noel Harrison and Stefanie Powers, who embodies the Ian Fleming–created April Dancer in the spin-off *The Girl from U.N.C.L.E.*

EVERETT

20TH CENTURY FOX/EVERETT

20TH CENTURY FOX/EVERETT

ALLAN GRANT

CO RENTMEESTER

TOP ROW: There were always beauties at hand in Dean Martin's four Matt Helm films between 1966 and '69 (left, with Ann-Margret), and in James Coburn's two turns as "our man" Flint in '66 and '67. These movies exist somewhere between Bond rip-offs and Bond parodies, which is particularly odd in the Helm instance since that series's producer, Irving Allen, told Ian Fleming back in the 1950s that his Bond novels were "not good enough for television." Bottom row: Female heroines got their day in the 1966 film *Modesty Blaise* (left, starring Monica Vitti) and even in the male-centric 1965 Bond-influenced renovation of the *Burke's Law* TV series as *Amos Burke: Secret Agent.* Gene Barry still starred as Burke, but Anne Francis (right) got her own show, *Honey West,* in which she was happy to deploy such gadgetry as tear-gas earrings and a garter-belt gas mask. Opposite: The most enduring of all Bond knockoff film series is unquestionably that starring actor Tony Ferrer (in white), the so-called James Bond of the Philippines. His character—Tony Falcon, Agent X44—first appeared in the 1965 film *G-2,* then subsequently in more than a dozen sequels. Agent X44 films, now comedies, were made as recently as 2007, with Ferrer guesting as a graybeard.

FX NETWORKS/EVERETT

EVERETT

CRYING FREEMAN PROD./KOBAL/ART RESOURCE, NY

JOHN BRAMLEY/WARNER BROS.

BERT CANN/CAMERA PRESS/REDUX

BEFORE DAVID NIVEN made the full-blown spoof *Casino Royale* in 1967, he sort of embodied the James Bond role that Ian Fleming had always thought him suited for in 1965's *Where the Spies Are.* On the opposite page, he romances the French actress Françoise Dorléac. His character's name was actually Jason Love in the film, and just by the way: Noel Harrison was in this one, too. Above, top left, is a cell from the contemporary TV animated spy series *Archer.* Top right are Diana Rigg and Patrick Macnee in the wonderful and long-running British series *The Avengers,* which actually predated the Bond film franchise—it began in 1961 and lasted until 1969—but, like *The Saint* and the American Amos Burke series, it took on Bondian overtones through the years. Rigg would go on to portray James Bond's only wife in *On Her Majesty's Secret Service,* then many better roles in an illustrious career. In the bottom row, left, is an incendiary scene from 1995's *Crying Freeman,* a French-Canadian film based on a Japanese comic strip about a lethal Chinese assassin who sheds tears every time he kills (and so sheds twice as many after this encounter). Above, right, are movie stars Val Kilmer and Robert Downey Jr. in a scene from *Kiss Kiss Bang Bang,* which sounds like the title of a 1960s James Bond knockoff but was in fact released in 2005.

THE REEL HISTORY

In 1964 the word in New York City's Times Square is: Bond is back! Forty-eight years later, as *Skyfall* arrives, it still is.

CASINO ROYALE [PART I]

As has been mentioned earlier in our book, the first movie adaptation of a Bond novel appeared on television in 1954, when *Casino Royale* was Americanized one year after its publication as a novel in England. As an episode in the CBS anthology series *Climax!*, it didn't create much of a stir at the time, but it has a certain cachet today. It was originally broadcast live and was believed lost for the longest time, but in 1981 a kinescope was found and is currently available on DVD as a bonus on the disc that includes the 1967 comedic version. (MGM finally bought up the rights to both of these "unofficial" films, as well as Sean Connery's renegade *Never Say Never Again*, and today markets the complete canon, flimflam and all.) *Casino Royale* is one of the rare episodes of *Climax!* that is commercially available today, another being an adaptation of Robert Louis Stevenson's *The Strange Case of Dr. Jekyll and Mr. Hyde* written by none other than Gore Vidal.

WHAT WOULD FLEMING THINK?

HE WAS A NEWLY successful writer of thrillers, so of course was thrilled in turn by a quick adaptation of his first book, especially since *Casino Royale* hadn't sold well in the American market. Having his austere Bond turned into a CIA agent called Jimmy probably amused as much as it rankled. No doubt the conflations of certain characters necessitated by the 48-minute running time seemed odd to Fleming.

CLASS ACTS

FOR SUCH A run-of-the-mill project (American television in the mid-1950s was becoming adept at churning out product to feed the beast, and in four years there were no fewer than 166 episodes of *Climax!*), *Casino Royale* featured personnel of pedigree. Le Chiffre was played by the legendary Peter Lorre (in the white dinner jacket, at right, during the torture scene—much toned down from the novel—with Barry Nelson as Bond in the tub). The music for the teleplay was composed by Jerry Goldsmith, who went on to score scores of TV shows and films (including five *Star Trek*s) and who won an Oscar for *The Omen*. Then of course there was Nelson himself, a fine actor, and also the coscreenwriter Charles Bennett. Bennett not only scripted Alfred Hitchcock classics of the 1930s when he and Hitch were still at home in England but went on to write *Curse of the Demon* (1957), *Voyage to the Bottom of the Sea* (1961) and *City in the Sea* (1965).

CBS PHOTO ARCHIVE/GETTY (2)

TOP SECRET

☞ **DO YOU REMEMBER** Byron Lee and the Dragonaires? The pioneering Jamaican ska band, who would back such as Jimmy Cliff on recordings, contributed several songs to the film and appeared as a house band at the hotel performing "Jump Up." The "Bond music" itself was, from the first, composed and orchestrated by Englishman John Barry—with the important caveat that Monty Norman was credited with the famous theme, after there was some discussion about who contributed which notes.

☞ **IT'S FITTING** that *Dr. No* was the initial foray into feature films: The novel was born, in 1956, as a screenplay—done by Fleming for what would have been a British television series entitled *Commander Jamaica*. When that didn't pan out, Fleming used his script as the basis for a book, sixth in the Bond series and published on March 31, 1958.

☞ **THERE IS EVIDENCE** that the producers wanted to really churn out these Bond films: The initial contract offered to Connery was for six films in just three years. He had recently had a bad experience with 20th Century Fox, and demurred, which certainly proved a good thing for moviegoers everywhere. Connery retained the liberty to play other roles, and the Bond frequency was reduced to one per year.

DR. NO

Obviously, it took a while for James Bond to make it to the big screen, and by the time he did Ian Fleming was a big success and his yearly thrillers were selling in big quantities on both sides of the pond. Following the American TV production of *Casino Royale* in 1954, there were overtures and even plans for more adaptations, but nothing happened for the longest time. In 1960, Canadian producer Harry Saltzman set his mind on Bond and approached Fleming. To make certain Saltzman would put considerable energy behind any project, Fleming asked a king's ransom: $50,000 for a six-month license to get something moving, and an additional $100,000 when a film was released. Saltzman drew a breath, said yes, and then partnered with coproducer Cubby Broccoli. *Dr. No* was chosen to be the first feature film. The talent search to "Find James Bond" yielded a few finalists, who auditioned for Saltzman, Broccoli and Fleming, and a leader emerged in male model Peter Anthony (a harbinger of George Lazenby!?), but he was ultimately nixed by Broccoli. The chosen one: Sean Connery.

WHAT'S UP, DOC?

JOSEPH WISEMAN, seen opposite at left with costars Sean Connery and Ursula Andress and, at right, insulated against his own poisonous malevolence, was not only not Asian, he really had little concept of what was going on. A native of Montreal, he was a veteran of the stage, praised for his turns in *King Lear, Uncle Vanya,* Clifford Odets's *Golden Boy* and Jean Anouilh's *The Lark.* "A life being enacted onstage is a thing of utter fascination to me," he once said. "And acting, it may begin out of vanity but you hope that it's taken over by something else. I hope I've climbed over the vanity hurdle." So he wasn't some villainous add-on, he was a thinking person's thespian. In movies, he had played opposite giants: Kirk Douglas in *Detective Story* and Marlon Brando in *Viva Zapata!* To him, *Dr. No,* for which the late Joseph Wiseman will forever be remembered, looked like a paycheck: "I had no idea what I was letting myself in for. I had no idea it would achieve the success it did. I know nothing about mysteries. I don't take to them. As far as I was concerned, I thought it might be just another grade-B Charlie Chan mystery."

EVERETT

UA/MPTVIMAGES

BOX OFFICE

BOFFO, considering it was the first. Released on May 8, 1963, it sold 19 million tickets in the United States, grossed $16,067,000 in the U.S. and $59,500,000 worldwide; converted to 2012 dollars, that equals $452,115,000—a solid hit by anyone's standards.

FUN IN THE SUN

FILMING IN PART in Ian Fleming's beloved Jamaica, hard by his estate Goldeneye, the *Dr. No* set was lighthearted, absent the kind of pressures that would eventually accrue on Bond productions, when expectations were set so high. This prevalent attitude infected the film, which director Terence Young and Sean Connery saw as much more comedic and less severe than Fleming's gripping novels.

GIFT FROM THE SEA

SO ONE DAY producers Broccoli and Saltzman are sifting through a sheaf of publicity shots of beautiful young women whose agents would like to have them be considered for the role of Honey Ryder, who would be—unbeknownst to all at the time—the original (and, many think, the quintessence) of a substantial sorority of Bond Girls. Suddenly, Broccoli pauses on a photo of Ursula Andress walking out of the surf. "Well," he says, "this is the girl, Harry." And indeed she was. Andress, seen here larking about with Connery on the set, was a Swiss actress about to make a substantial splash—and then a couple of career mistakes. Her iconic scene where she rises from the Caribbean Sea in a white bikini was an entrance equal to Connery's "Bond . . . James Bond." (By the way, Ursula's swimwear sold at auction in 2001 for nearly $60,000.) Despite having her role entirely dubbed—she had a Germanic accent—Andress won a Golden Globe as Most Promising Newcomer in 1964, which today seems laughable. She posed nude for *Playboy* magazine the following year, explaining her rationale: "Because I'm beautiful." Then she said goodbye to Broccoli and Saltzman forevermore by agreeing to appear in the Bond parody *Casino Royale* in 1967. She has been heard from since, but not often.

UNITED ARTISTS/GETTY

WHAT WOULD FLEMING THINK?

WE KNOW he didn't think Connery was right for the role, we know he wanted a more cerebral and brutal Bond and we know he had a nice time visiting the set (opposite). We know he was happy with the initial checks mailed by Saltzman and Co. and then thrilled with the subsequent ones after the movie opened, not to mention the booming sales of his books. Commander Fleming was now on board.

FROM RUSSIA WITH LOVE

There was little doubt after *Dr. No* that James Bond would return to theaters, and would again be personified by Sean Connery. Crucially, director Terence Young returned for a second turn as well, and he and Connery refined their winking vision of Ian Fleming's superspy, establishing it forevermore. Add-ons, including cool toys deployed by Bond and his SPECTRE nemeses, were firmly installed as de rigueur parts of the Bond formula as well, and still today Rosa Klebb's blade-hidden-in-the-shoe is revered by Bond fans. (In *From Russia with Love*, the actor Desmond Llewelyn as Major Boothroyd, Head of Q Section—the British military intelligence gadgetry unit—stamps himself an early Hall of Fame associate along with Bernard Lee as M and Lois Maxwell as Miss Moneypenny; the character Felix Leiter is on hiatus after *Dr. No*, but will return to the series, though Jack Lord, the original Leiter, will be banished after a contract dispute.) *Russia* remains today among the most thrilling Bond entries: a true spy caper. Many consider it the very best Bond of all.

BOX OFFICE

BOFFO, and certainly reason to forge ahead. A total of 26.8 million tickets sold in the U.S. translated to U.S. grosses of $24.8 million, up more than 50 percent over *Dr. No.* Worldwide grosses of $78,900,000 would equate to $591,690,000 today, and would rival the Roger Moore films and beat Pierce Brosnan's in approximate success.

WHAT WOULD FLEMING THINK?

A POINT TO BE MADE HERE: During the time that Fleming was alive for the production of four sanctioned Bond movies, including the TV offering, filmmakers were actually adapting the books. They weren't just attaching a Fleming (or Flemingesque) title to an entirely unrelated plotline; they were paying attention to source material. *Russia* was a Fleming movie, and the reviews following its October 1963 release were terrific.

- **LIFE MAGAZINE** was talking with U.S. President John F. Kennedy, and he allowed that *From Russia with Love* was one of his 10 favorite books. This made news, and producers Saltzman and Broccoli, sniffing free publicity, chose *Russia,* Fleming's fifth novel in the series—published in 1957 and with events set in the summer of '54—as their *Dr. No* follow-up. On November 20, 1963, JFK screened the film at the White House. This was the last movie he ever saw, as he left for Dallas shortly thereafter.

- **DESPERATE TO COME UP** with a successor to Ursula Andress, the producers sent out a press release summoning a "voluptuous, young Greta Garbo." Name actresses were considered, but ultimately the Italian model and Miss Universe runner-up Daniela Bianchi (seen on these pages) was chosen (reportedly with Sean Connery's urging).

- **ANOTHER NOTE ON BIANCHI:** Part of her screen test was a session on the bed with a Connery stand-in (the photo on the opposite page is from the rehearsal, and that's the real Bond). After her selection, this horizontal audition before the director and producers was legendarily the most important test a prospective Bond Girl needed to pass.

CLASS ACTS

THE JAMES BOND FILMS have in their 50 years featured a large number of famous folk (or folk who would go on to greater fame) who have dropped by to portray heroes or villains—people from cultural icons of the moment like Grace Jones (May Day in *A View to a Kill*) to eternal legends like Orson Welles (the villain Le Chiffre in the comedy version of *Casino Royale*). In *From Russia with Love,* a semi-legendary Austrian actress/singer and a British fellow destined for great cinematic things were memorable baddies. Do you recognize the actor behind the grim visage of assassin Donald Grant? It is a young, buff, blond-on-blond Robert Shaw, who would later play Henry VIII in *A Man for All Seasons* and, indelibly, the shark-hunter Quint in *Jaws*. His female accomplice here is none other than the Tony Award–winning (for her husband Kurt Weill's *The Threepenny Opera*), Oscar-nominated (for *The Roman Spring of Mrs. Stone*) Lotte Lenya as the sadistic Rosa Klebb. Lenya—yes, she gets a shout-out in the "Mack the Knife" lyrics as belted by Louis Armstrong and later Bobby Darin— was an enormous theatrical and classical music figure well before she accepted the role in a Bond film, but because of her classic last scene when she is trying to kick Sean Connery with the poisoned toe spike that had been hidden in her shoe (she's eventually shot dead by the Daniela Bianchi character, Tatiana Romanova), Lenya was always remembered by some for one thing only. She said that for the rest of her days the first thing people did after being introduced to her was to look at her shoes.

THE SPECTER OF SPECTRE

IN THE BOND NOVELS, our favorite British agent fought the Soviet Union's SMERSH regularly, but opposed the international crime conglomerate focused on world domination, SPECTRE (SPecial Executive for Counterintelligence, Terrorism, Revenge and Extortion), only a few times, most prominently, in 1961's *Thunderball*. In the Bond movies, by contrast, SPECTRE was a fixture: Dr. Julius No worked for the organization, as did Rosa Klebb and (again in this picture, getting his comeuppance) Donald Grant. SPECTRE's evil overlord Ernst Stavro Blofeld makes his first appearance, a brief one, in *From Russia with Love,* and meatier roles are ahead.

SCENE STEALER

IF LOTTE LENYA was forevermore remembered for a custom-made shoe, then Shirley Eaton, who made the cover of LIFE magazine in her golden girl get-up, has in her past a film career that is all asterisk: She was the British actress who played Jill Masterson, who suffered death by "skin suffocation" (a Fleming invention, scientifically impossible) after being painted head-to-toe by Goldfinger's henchman, Oddjob. Eaton, here with Connery and opposite in the midst of her hour-and-a-half-long gilding session with makeup artist Paul Rabiger, was apparently so convincing in her death scene that an urban myth grew that she had actually been killed during filming. In fact, she retired from acting not long after to raise her family. She had a long marriage that ended with her husband's death.

GOLDFINGER

Everything about it was golden: The song, the soundtrack, the number of tickets sold, the general furor—if furor can have a hue. MI6 and CIA agents and SMERSH veterans couldn't wait to see *Goldfinger,* and neither could anyone else. This was one of those event openings that we have become used to, along the lines of *Toy Story 3* or *Harry Potter and the Deathly Hallows: Part II.* A successful series has built a fan base, the producers know they have a terrific movie in the hopper, and suddenly all the world is queuing up. Back in 1964, such excitement over the latest installment in a film franchise was novel, and the rules that have led us to worldwide midnight screenings were just being written. In looking back, we now know that mistakes were nearly made—Harry Saltzman tried to kill the theme song, for goodness' sake!— but in the end, *Goldfinger* got just about everything right. Needless to say, it was richly rewarded for this. It reaped the gold.

A BOND-WORTHY VILLAIN

GERT FRÖBE, who played Auric Goldfinger as he engineered a caper to knock off Fort Knox and make away with enough bullion to sate even his outsize appetites, was a German actor whose accent was so thick that his dialogue was dubbed (retaining a hint of the Germanic). Fröbe's career is rife with Bond six-degrees-of-separation associations. To mention two: Among the movies in which he starred were *Three Penny Opera*—the music for which was composed by Kurt Weill, husband of Lotte Lenya (*From Russia with Love*'s Rosa Klebb), and for which Lenya, on a New York City stage, won her Tony Award—and *Chitty Chitty Bang Bang*, based on Ian Fleming's children's book and produced by Bond series chieftain Cubby Broccoli. As for *Chitty*, it was a musical adaptation and a hit in 1968, featuring, besides Fröbe, *Mary Poppins* veterans Dick Van Dyke and composers Richard and Robert Sherman. *Time* magazine said its songs had "all the rich melodic variety of an automobile horn," but that nonetheless the family-fare movie was welcome relief in an era rife with the kinds of films the *Goldfinger*-spurred Bond craze encouraged: "At a time when violence and sex are the dual sellers at the box office, *Chitty Chitty Bang Bang* looks better than it is simply because it's not not all all bad bad."

UA/MPTVIMAGES

TOP SECRET

☛ **DIRECTOR GUY HAMILTON** wanted to use a real laser for the famous scene in which Bond is nearly cleft in twain by Goldfinger. That was deemed too dangerous, which no doubt relieved Sean Connery. Instead, an acetylene torch concealed beneath the table cut through from below; the sparks were real, and Connery's sweat was surely due in part to the heat. A dummy laser above created the light beam.

☛ **ODDJOB'S FORD RANCHERO** truck was even more of a miracle vehicle than Bond's customized Aston Martin DB5 sports car. The pickup had no problem with the weight of the crushed Lincoln Continental when the compacted remains were lowered into its bed. In reality, the Lincoln rubble, even without Mr. Solo's body weight included, would have been five times too heavy for the Ford.

☛ **MICHAEL CAINE** was the first person besides composer John Barry to hear the music for the famous *Goldfinger* theme. How's that? Barry was already at work on *The Ipcress File*, which would make Caine a star with his performance as spy Harry Palmer, and Caine was staying with Barry for a time while the composer did mop-up work on the Bond film.

GADGETS AND GIRLS

THE EARLY BOOKS had been all but devoid of gadgetry, and the coolest stuff was in the hands of the bad guys, and that was the case with the first two feature films as well. *Goldfinger,* and particularly Bond's car, changed all that. The idea of the Bond Girl underwent a sea change, too—and a template was drawn that would prove enduring. There could be several girls per movie of different kinds, including women brought over from the dark side. Both Shirley Eaton's Jill Masterson (this page, and opposite, bottom, joking after the big scene, and proving she's not really dead) and Honor Blackman's Pussy Galore (opposite, top) turned on Goldfinger, thanks to Bond's charms. As to how to get that name—Pussy—by the censors, publicist Tom Carlile had an idea: Before the film opened he sent Blackman to the London premiere of *Move Over, Darling* and made sure she was photographed with Prince Philip. He coaxed his pals at the *Daily Mail* into running a photo with the caption headline "Pussy and the Prince." No public outcry ensued, and the censors allowed the original Ian Fleming name to stand, paving the way for Plenty O'Toole, Holly Goodhead and all the others.

WHAT WOULD
FLEMING THINK?

HE VISITED THE SET in April 1964 and died in August of that year at age 56. The movie, a global sensation beyond anything he had realized with his books or the first two feature films, was released in the United Kingdom in September and in the U.S. three days before Christmas. Maybe he would have wished he had taken better care of himself, and lived to enjoy the transcendent fame and great fortune. But then, you read the scenes he wrote with horror about aging Florida retirees in *Live and Let Die,* and you think: Maybe not.

BOX OFFICE

BEYOND BOFFO. *Goldfinger* was the game-changer, there is no question about that. Using all of the good things Terence Young had invented—the pizzazz and the sly humor—director Guy Hamilton delivered a masterwork. The audience was ready for it, having been well primed by a host of magazine articles. (Just a side note: Our sister Time Inc. publication *Sports Illustrated* sent a reporter along with LIFE photographer Loomis Dean to England to do a piece on the terrifically tense golf match between Goldfinger and Bond, where Connery got some pointers from Bernard Lee, above, before the shoot. By the way, the best athlete on the course that day was Goldfinger's caddie, Oddjob, played by Harold Sakata, who had been an Olympic silver medalist weightlifter and was even then a well-known pro wrestler.) Soon after the mania hit Times Square in New York City (opposite), the numbers started ticking over rapidly: more than 50 million tickets sold in the U.S. for a gross total of more than $50 million, converting to $378,270,000 in 2012 dollars; a worldwide gross of $124,900,000 converts to $924,570,000, which places it second, all-time, as the biggest Bond film ever. And what was the first? Please turn the page.

MIRRORPIX/EVERETT

UA/MPTVIMAGES (3)

THUNDERBALL

T he 1965 entry in the Bond series had everything to lose: *Goldfinger* had set an impossibly high bar. So Broccoli and Saltzman proceeded with purpose. Question One: Which book? *Thunderball* had been their original choice, over *Dr. No*, to launch the series, but there had been complications. Even before *Thunderball* had become a novel, elements of it had been kicked around in a collaborative screenplay project involving Ian Fleming, Kevin McClory and Jack Whittingham. McClory started claiming that much of *Thunderball*, including the inventions of SPECTRE and the fiendish Blofeld, belonged to him, and Broccoli and Saltzman walked away—at the time. Now they wanted *Thunderball* on the big screen, and made a deal with McClory: He'd be a third producer on the film and in turn would let Eon Productions use SPECTRE and Blofeld now and for a dozen more years. That's why the evil genius and his criminal enterprise disappear from the "official" series after *Diamonds Are Forever*. As for *Thunderball:* With *Goldfinger*'s lead-in, Connery and director Terence Young back, Blofeld on board and a slew of new toys, it couldn't miss. It didn't.

TOP SECRET

☞ **THE GREAT SHIRLEY BASSEY,** having hit the heights with her recording of the *Goldfinger* theme song, recorded the John Barry–Leslie Bricusse song "Mr. Kiss Kiss Bang Bang" as the *Thunderball* theme (Dionne Warwick recorded a second version). But the producers wanted a song with the title in it, and Tom Jones was available to sing the new tune; he held the last note so long he fainted. Today, the singers, both Welsh, have been dubbed by the queen of England Dame Shirley and Sir Tom.

☞ **THE JETPACK** was one of the ideas in the mid-1960s that everyone was sure represented the future; the *Jetsons* cartoon show was no doubt responsible. All such ideas were used in Bond films eventually, and in *Thunderball,* 007 employs the Bell rocket belt (right), supplied by Q, to escape two gunmen after killing SPECTRE agent No. 6, Colonel Jacques Bouvar. A jetpack was also used in 2002's *Die Another Day*— it's definitely a Bond Hall of Fame gadget—but a decade thereafter, it has yet to make its mark in our daily life.

☞ **BOND CYNICISM** had begun to set in. From the *Time* magazine review: "Though *From Russia with Love* remains the liveliest Bond opera to date, *Thunderball* is by all odds the most spectacular. Its script hasn't a morsel of genuine wit, but Bond fans, who are preconditioned to roll in the aisles when their hero merely asks a waiter to bring some beluga caviar and Dom Perignon '55, will probably never notice. They are switched on by a legend that plays straight to the senses, and its colors are primary."

BOX OFFICE

BEYOND BOFFO AND BELIEF. We'll get to the conversions, but focus on this for a second: *Thunderball* sold 74.8 million tickets in the U.S., nearly half again as many as *Goldfinger* and about three times as many as the most popular Roger Moore, Pierce Brosnan or Daniel Craig pictures. The worldwide gross of $141,200,000 translates to $1,028,640,000 in 2012 dollars, making *Thunderball* the equivalent of a billion-dollar picture today. That's rarefied air.

EVERETT

GAMMA-KEYSTONE/GETTY

A BOND-WORTHY VILLAIN

EMILIO LARGO was SPECTRE's No. 2 to Ernst Stavro Blofeld, and in *Thunderball* he was the main bad guy as he masterminded a daring bombnap. The climax of the movie is a spectacular undersea battle/ballet between Largo's forces and our hero's (*Thunderball*'s team won the special-effects Oscar). The Sicilian actor Adolfo Celi played Largo, and for a second time in a row the principal villain's voice was dubbed due to a thick European accent. Two years after *Thunderball*, Celi made the egregious error of appearing in the Bond spoof *Operation Kid Brother*, which starred, yes, Sean Connery's kid brother, Neil.

CASINO ROYALE [PART II]

As we see elsewhere in our book, there were lots of imitations, farces and spoofs made in hopes of cashing in on the Bond craze, especially during the post-*Goldfinger* mania in the 1960s. (Weirdly, the most successful was the *Austin Powers* franchise, launched decades later, when most folks this side of Mike Myers thought sending up James Bond was hopelessly passé.) Singular among the knockoffs and satires was the 1967 version of *Casino Royale* because it was actually based on an Ian Fleming novel (sort of), starred an A-list cast, including the man who might've been the "real" Bond if Fleming had had his way (David Niven), and is still watchable today (kind of), even if best appreciated as an artifact. How had this bizarro undertaking come to pass? Well, *Casino Royale*'s rights had come into the possession of producer Charles K. Feldman, and after he was rebuffed on a partnership overture by Broccoli and Saltzman, and by Sean Connery to star, he turned the project into a spoof. One problem: Many of the stars who had signed on hadn't been told.

WHAT WOULD FLEMING THINK?

WELL, HE WOULD HAVE BEEN HORRIFIED, of course. The plot, such as it was, has five agents take on the name "James Bond" in an effort to mess with SMERSH—five in addition to Niven's Sir James Bond. This was the first film to depart so egregiously from what had been written. Some future productions would take the titles and ignore the books altogether.

EVERETT (2)

CLASS ACTS

IF THE MOVIE WAS, ummm, stupid—and it surely was—many of its lead actors and other personnel were anything but. One of its five credited directors was John Huston, who back in the early 1960s had wondered about making a Bond movie starring Cary Grant. Woody Allen not only acted as one of the ersatz Bonds, he contributed some (uncredited) writing, as did Huston and Orson Welles, who also costarred. Niven, at left with Angela Scoular and above in the white suit with Joanna Pettet in the foreground, was an Oscar winner. We have mentioned Deborah Kerr, and then there was Peter Sellers and Jacqueline Bisset as Giovanna Goodthighs and William Holden and Burt Bacharach's music and . . .

WHEN EGOS COLLIDE

WOODY ALLEN, who had made his Hollywood bow as screenwriter for Charles K. Feldman's 1965 *What's New Pussycat* (in which he also played a small role), wrote many of his own bits for Feldman's *Casino Royale* (above, far right), but largely stayed above the constant fray on the set. After all, he was only 30 during filming, and deferred to his legendary elders . . . who fought like cats. Orson Welles reportedly insisted on having magic tricks written into his portrayal of Le Chiffre, which for some reason rubbed Peter Sellers (opposite, with Andress) the wrong way. Things got so bad between Welles and Sellers that they needed stand-ins—not for stunt scenes but simply for when the two men were supposed to be facing each other across a table. Sellers had people fired from the production, then was fired himself in turn. Would that there were a behind-the-scenes movie of the filming of *Casino Royale*. That would be a flick worth watching.

BETTER THAN DESERVED. The film went way over budget; some reports said $12 million in all. (Producer Feldman bumped into Connery at a cocktail party and conceded he would have saved money by just paying the Scot's million-dollar asking price.) And the running time ballooned to an excruciating two hours, 11 minutes. But in 1967 there was an audience for all things Bond: $22,750,000 in U.S. grosses, nearly twice that worldwide. Orson Welles attributed the film's success to the poster of the naked girl with the psychedelic body paint.

YOU ONLY LIVE TWICE

So much seemed to be precisely the same—Sean Connery as Bond, Bernard Lee as M, Desmond Llewelyn as Q, Lois Maxwell as Moneypenny, a high-tech subplot (space capsules highjacked in outer space!), sensational Bond Girls, sinister Asians, John Barry's music, a cool theme song (Nancy Sinatra on vocals). And there were new treats: the pleasure of Donald Pleasence's company as Blofeld, the first time that character was allowed to truly strut his vile stuff onscreen, replete with the scary scar and the equally disquieting Persian cat; a screenplay by none other than Roald Dahl (who meantime was adapting Ian Fleming's *Chitty Chitty Bang Bang* as a family film); and finally the first 007 film premiere attended by the queen of England. So *You Only Live Twice* was sent to the theaters with all due fanfare. But there was something the slightest bit wrong. A lassitude, perhaps: a sense of having been there, done that. Or maybe it was finally proving true: James Bond, long suspected of not being quite right for the changing times of the 1960s, wasn't made for 1967. Much of the old gang would reunite a few years later in *Diamonds Are Forever,* but here they looked like they needed a vacation.

BOX OFFICE

DOWN BUT NOT OUT. The film sold fewer than half as many tickets at U.S. theaters than had *Thunderball,* but interestingly that lesser figure—36.2 million—is nevertheless nearly 10 million more than any Bond film since. Its converted worldwide gross of $766,760,000 places it third all-time behind *Goldfinger* and *Thunderball,* but still: At the time, it seemed the bloom might be coming off the rose.

WHAT WOULD FLEMING THINK?

IN THIS INSTANCE, what Fleming might think is a hard question to answer. When he wrote *You Only Live Twice,* he was already quite ill. It is uneven, not the best, but it includes that fascinating and premature 1962 London *Times* obituary of Bond, and it is intriguing in other ways. It follows directly on from the murder of James Bond's wife by the arch criminal Blofeld, which occurs at the end of *On Her Majesty's Secret Service.* Producing *Twice* first as a movie, before establishing the grief and waywardness in Bond that prompts M to send him on a mission to Japan, probably would not have made sense to Fleming. Oddly, he may have found the relative lack of zip to the cinematic proceedings as a good fit for Bond's personal malaise during *You Only Live Twice.* At the end of the day, personally, he might well have seen the writing on the wall, as this was the first Bond movie to largely ignore most of what he had written in terms of plot and the evolving nature of his main character.

EVERETT (2)

☛ **FOR SOME REASON,** in *You Only Live Twice*, James Bond did not pilot any kind of vehicle—first time ever.

☛ **THE SOUNDTRACK,** probably linked to the film's subdued performance, didn't sell well, but has since come to be regarded as a John Barry masterwork. Shirley Bassey covered the theme song many years after the film's release.

☛ **BRITISH ACTOR CHARLES GRAY,** seen here dead on his feet, is ill-fated Bond ally Dikko Henderson in *You Only Live Twice*. In *Diamonds Are Forever*, he will be promoted to the role of awful genius Ernst Stavro Blofeld and will acquit himself ably, even in the considerable wake of Donald Pleasence and Telly Savalas.

ON HER MAJESTY'S SECRET SERVICE

Because this production is so associated with the casting of George Lazenby after the Australian model (opposite) had won a talent-search contest staged by Broccoli and Saltzman, a contest that drew some 400 entrants after Sean Connery retired (for the first time) from the Bond role, other non-Lazenby aspects of the film have gone missing. *On Her Majesty's Secret Service* was blessed with a great plot, which was sufficiently preserved in its translation from page to screen. The film featured one of the most distinguished actresses ever to accept the appellation Bond Girl in Diana Rigg (seen and discussed below), and it honored her (in a way) by allowing her to become Mrs. Bond (just before she was murdered). It featured, as well, a second great performance as Blofeld when Telly Savalas followed Donald Pleasence in the juicy role. But also, it had a running time of two hours, 20 minutes, which is indicative of several things: Bond, even if it was still getting many things right, was bloating on jokes and gimmickry; Bond was losing sight of what worked best; Bond was, in its first post-Connery outing, more than a little bit lost.

BOX OFFICE

FLOP. Its worldwide gross, adjusted for inflation, was barely over $400 million, which wasn't as much as even the first film's and wouldn't be bottomed in the "official" series until 1985's *A View to a Kill,* Roger Moore's seventh and last Bond movie. In the U.S., *On Her Majesty's Secret Service* sold 16 million tickets, another low record that would stand until 1985.

CLASS ACT

BOND LORE HOLDS, accurately, that George Lazenby's film career all but evaporated when he chose not to re-up for future installments in the series. Diana Rigg, too, made only the one Bond film, *On Her Majesty's Secret Service,* but her résumé did nothing but extend thereafter. Born in 1938 in Yorkshire, England, she was already a big star in her native land when she accepted the role in 1969's *Secret Service.* She had performed many times onstage throughout the 1960s, starring in everything from Shakespeare on down, and had gained fame as the jumpsuited Mrs. Emma Peel in the television series *The Avengers.* That show was picked up by many stations in the States, too, but Rigg has said that a principal intention in becoming a Bond Girl was to raise her profile in America. This she did, and then proceeded upon a career dotted with triumphs in the West End and on Broadway, on the big screen and the small (memorably, opposite Laurence Olivier in *King Lear,* and then in *Rebecca,* for which she won an Emmy). She was made a Dame Commander of the Order of the British Empire in 1994, so the Bond series has two Sirs, in Connery and Moore, and two Dames, in Rigg and Judi Dench, who has assayed the role of M in the most recent films.

DIAMONDS ARE FOREVER

This is one of the more fascinating entries in our Reel History. There's little question that, less than a decade old, the franchise was at a crisis point. If Broccoli and Saltzman didn't want to admit it, their distribution partners at United Artists were eager to, and they said, essentially: Pay him. The "him" was of course Sean Connery, who, moving about in the movie world—unsigned—was a solution, a fix-all, an antidote, a stopgap—crassly put, a plug to their leaking ship. He surely couldn't be counted on to represent "the future," if ever a decades-long future was then imagined. But the producers needed at least a bridge to that future, and as the 1970s dawned and Lazenby bid farewell, there seemed only one answer if the series wanted to stay on course. Rather wonderfully, when Connery returned to the role, the production took on the trappings of a happy reunion, and *Diamonds Are Forever* has a spark that *You Only Live Twice* was sorely lacking. Sean was older, sure, and softer in physique, but Bond's audience was, too. Before this whole thing had to be blown up and rebuilt, one more romp.

CONNERY'S LAST (TRUE) HURRAH. He would raise his graying head once more in 1983's "unofficial" *Never Say Never Again,* but *Diamonds* returned the great Scot to comfortable confines, and the audience returned too: It sold over 10 million more tickets in the U.S. than did *On Her Majesty's Secret Service* and made a converted worldwide gross of $657,270,000—a take that would be bettered by two of seven Roger Moore films.

CLASS ACTS

THE CONNERY BOND MOVIES, as opposed to those starring, say, Timothy Dalton or Daniel Craig, have always had a comic-book aspect. In the more somber Bond films, for instance, the goofy Fleming-inspired character names seem a disconnect. Happy to be back together, that old gang of ours—M, Q, Moneypenny, *Goldfinger*'s director Guy Hamilton—had a gay old time in *Diamonds Are Forever,* and their esprit de corps was shared by newcomers called Tiffany Case, Plenty O'Toole and the memorable (and *really* gay) Mr. Kidd and Mr. Wint. Bernard Lee, Desmond Llewelyn and Lois Maxwell were certainly happy to have former colleague Connery back at MI6, and Jill St. John (opposite, as Case), Lana Wood (Natalie's kid sister, who played O'Toole) and none other than Jimmy Dean (as a Howard Hughes–type villain named Willard Whyte) chewed all available scenery in their supporting roles. The actors who played Messrs. Kidd and Wint deserve naming, too: Putter Smith and Bruce Glover, forevermore members of the Bond Bad Guys Roll of Dishonor.

DANJAQ/EON/UA/KOBAL/ART RESOURCE, NY

TERRY O'NEILL/GETTY

WHAT WOULD FLEMING THINK?

HE MIGHT'VE BEEN AMUSED by all of the outer space stuff, and he might not have been. Remember: This well-received novel, with Bond focused on the diamond-smuggling pipeline from Sierra Leone to Las Vegas, was published in 1956, well before even Sputnik. This was an earthbound narrative. Interestingly, *Diamonds Are Forever*'s first adaptation was as a Fleming-sanctioned comic strip that ran in the *Daily Express* (and in syndication) in 1959 and '60.

ROLE OF A LIFETIME

FOR A FEW YEARS, Sean Connery was considered for everything. There was the thought that he would be the perfect Captain von Trapp in *The Sound of Music* (but imagining a more perfect von Trapp than Christopher Plummer, now, is impossible). Later, in the 1980s, he won his Oscar for *The Untouchables*, but he always felt he could have won for the wonderful 1975 John Huston film *The Man Who Would Be King.* For all of his marvelous performances and versatility, he was the perfect Bond, and Bond was his perfect role—whether he liked the fact or not. He owned it, and owns it still.

WHAT NOW?

CONNERY, NAPPING on the set, hardly sleepwalked his way through *Diamonds Are Forever:* He earned his hefty fee, a considerable chunk of which went to charity in Scotland (better there than in Cubby Broccoli's well-stuffed wallet, Connery figured). Yes, he worked for his reward, but now he would leave Bond for a second time. The producers required a solution that might last longer than a single film. Roger Moore, who had been considered earlier, was now free of his TV show *The Saint* and prepared to ride to the rescue.

🔫 **"I WAS THE ONLY** Bond Girl who was accidental," the stunning Jane Seymour, who played the stunning Solitaire, told *People* magazine in 1983, a decade after making *Live and Let Die.* She, at age 21, had said she was not interested, ready to join a principled club including Raquel Welch, Catherine Deneuve, Faye Dunaway and others who had just said no. But the Bond folks called back, and Seymour realized "I had no money and only one good coat." She signed, but later lamented: "I've spent my life living down that part."

🔫 **PAUL MCCARTNEY,** who cowrote the theme song with his wife Linda, brought Beatles producer George Martin in to compose the film's score.

🔫 **TO SHOW HIS BOND WAS DIFFERENT** from Connery's, Moore never wore a hat, drank bourbon instead of martinis, smoked cigars instead of cigarettes and used a Magnum handgun, not a Walther.

LIVE AND LET DIE

hough the producers were prepared to move on from the Connery era, they made him a final, astounding offer of $5.5 million for yet another go. Sean demurred, and later was gallant, calling Moore "an ideal Bond." In many ways he was: He had personality, charisma, great charm. Bond's filmmakers, even as they allowed Moore to put his own stamp on the role, tried to cocoon him in ways the audience would find comforting, with Bernard Lee as M, Lois Maxwell as Moneypenny, and Guy Hamilton of *Goldfinger* and *Diamonds Are Forever* back at the helm. They began to pump up the thrills—soaring boats and such—and there's an irony here: Even as they embarked on the gadget-happy Moore era, the character Q went temporarily missing. One story is: The actor Desmond Llewelyn had a prior commitment, and by the time he had freed up enough time for Bond, Q was written out of *Live and Let Die*. A second account has it that Q was cut because the producers thought too much was being made of all the gadgets. Llewelyn was reportedly sad not to be included, but was later elated when fans demanded him back.

EVERETT

DANJAQ/EON/UA/KOBAL/ART RESOURCE, NY

WHAT WOULD FLEMING THINK?

ROGER MOORE'S BOND would have driven the author crazy. His obvious affection for dinner jackets and appreciation of the glamorous locales in which he found himself was of a piece with the written Bond. His constant wise-cracking and bad-joke-making would have left Fleming cringing. The performance was predictable: Many traits and tics, including the debonair insouciance and arched eyebrow, were imported wholesale from Moore's TV role on *The Saint*.

THE MAN WITH THE GOLDEN GUN

This was, in 1974, Guy Hamilton's fourth and final James Bond film, and this is both a good and a bad thing. He did make four, and those, added to Terence Young's three (among the first nine Eon films), got the series off to a rip-roaring start. Also: Based upon the quality of *The Man with the Golden Gun*, it's probably good that there wasn't a fifth Hamilton movie. But it is nevertheless sad that the man who made *Goldfinger* would depart with a considerably lesser offering. Watching *The Man with the Golden Gun* today, an inescapable conclusion is that after *Live and Let Die* launched the Roger Moore era successfully, all concerned felt the prudent thing to do was to paint by numbers: this many bikinis, check; this many outrageous stunts (maybe add one or two), check; this many stupid double entendres, check; drag in a couple of contemporary themes (in this case, the 1970s energy crisis and the martial arts craze), check, check and double-check. Then simply open the ticket booths. Doesn't always work that way.

BOX OFFICE

A WAKE-UP CALL. The people in line (well, the lines weren't very long) let the producers know that they couldn't just plop Bond ingredients into a blender and have a megahit every time out. Ticket sales in the U.S. were barely half of the first Roger Moore film, and the worldwide take was off by a fifth (nearly $200 million in today's dollars).

TOP SECRET

☞ **ALICE COOPER,** of all people, wrote a theme song for the film, but the producers opted for a John Barry composition with truly stupid (and downright dirty) lyrics by Don Black. This was recorded by Lulu. Cooper included his own tune on his 1973 Top 10 album, *Muscle of Love.*

☞ **ANOTHER MUSICAL NOTE:** Bond-veteran Barry wrote the film's score in three weeks and it showed: Not even the composer liked it. "It's the one I hate the most," Barry later said. "It just never happened for me."

☞ **THE MOORE-ERA GIMMICKRY**—the dastardly Scaramanga has a flying car in this one, to chase *Live and Let Die*'s flying boat—was being noticed. "Overtricky, uninspired," wrote Jay Cocks in *Time* magazine about how the franchise was going wrong. "[T]hese exercises show the strain of stretching fantasy well past wit."

DANJAQ/EON/UA/KOBAL/ART RESOURCE, NY (2)

BOND-WORTHY VILLAINS

MUCH ABOUT THE MOVIE was forgettable. Certainly Britt Ekland was no all-star Bond Girl, and if her fellow Swedish model Maud Adams made a better impression in a similar role, she would be better still as the title character in 1983's *Octopussy*. But Christopher Lee as Francisco Scaramanga, the man with the golden gun (opposite page, and also here, left, dueling with Moore), and Hervé Villechaize as Nick Nack, Scaramanga's dwarf servant and accomplice (his silhouette here in the foreground), were memorable. This was a good thing, for the casting of Lee could have been deemed favoritism, despite his strong pedigree in vampire films: He was Ian Fleming's cousin and golfing companion. The story goes that Fleming had nominated Lee as Dr. No, and the second part of the story is that maybe he forgot to tell the producers. Anyway, when Jack Palance passed on Scaramanga, Lee got the gig, and everyone was acquitted. Lee went on to immortalize another evildoer filed in the Movies Bad Guy Section under *S: Saruman*, in *The Lord of the Rings* trilogy and upcoming *Hobbit* films.

ROGER MOORE (below) rather hoped his *Spy Who Loved Me* costar would be Brigitte Bardot, but it wound up being another BB: Barbara Bach, a stunning beauty whose résumé was heavy with spaghetti westerns. She (seen on the opposite page, left) was a real asset to the film, and it boosted her career. On the set of *Caveman*, she met her costar and future husband, Ringo Starr, and they continue to make sweet music together.

THE 1977 FILM is best remembered for two of its players: Bach, and Richard Kiel, the seven-foot-two-and-a-half-inch actor who portrayed the steel-dentured Jaws (opposite, right) to such effect that he was invited back for the Bond follow-up *Moonraker*. It is perhaps interesting that Kiel—so visually useful, particularly as a henchman—had earlier guested on the Bond-influenced U.S. television series *The Man from U.N.C.L.E.*, *Honey West* and *I Spy*.

THE DIRECTOR LEWIS GILBERT, who had made *You Only Live Twice*, returned (and he would return again for *Moonraker*). Freed from having to adapt anything, he and his screenwriters made a crackerjack entertainment from whole cloth involving nuclear submarines, the KGB and other elements. The success of *The Spy Who Loved Me* surely emboldened Bond's producers with the idea that they no longer needed Ian Fleming source material. Big-name stars might help.

BOX OFFICE

BOFFO. Quite a comeback after *The Man with the Golden Gun*. Suffice it to say: The adjusted worldwide gross of *The Spy Who Loved Me*, $702 million, would place it fourth all-time among Bond films, after Sean Connery's middle-'60s big three: *Goldfinger*, *Thunderball* and *You Only Live Twice*. Roger Moore's job security at MI6 got a boost.

THE SPY WHO LOVED ME

The ultimate rarity: a successful movie based upon (no matter how loosely) a novel so bad that even its author sought to disown it. Ian Fleming in the earliest 1960s got it in his head, perhaps after too many shaken martinis, to write a Bond book from the standpoint of—in fact, in the voice of—a young woman. The novel, 10th in the series, was very short, sexually explicit, barely plotted and a grievous disappointment to the author's fans. Fleming quickly admitted the error of his ways. He moved to have a paperback version in the U.K. blocked, and occasionally said he wasn't jesting in the book's prologue when he wrote that he had found the manuscript and had simply decided to facilitate its publication. When he sold film rights to the bulk of his books to Saltzman and Broccoli, he made sure the action of *The Spy Who Loved Me* was not included, only the title. This was okay with them, and when Eon Productions got around to making the movie in 1976, the name—and two memorable henchmen, including one who would become immortal as Jaws—was all they took.

WHAT WOULD FLEMING THINK?

"OFF THE HOOK," that's what he would think. As mentioned above, in the few final years of his life after writing *The Spy Who Loved Me* in 1961, he tried to run away from the thing. If these filmmakers had taken his provocative title and had modeled one of his characters into a memorable screen villain named Jaws, and then had draped these few morsels in a larger, successful entertainment, well, he probably would have said: "Whew!"

MOONRAKER

Certainly no one was getting fired after the success of *The Spy Who Loved Me*. Roger Moore was back, director Lewis Gilbert was back, even Jaws was back. It is interesting to note: The events of *Moonraker*, in the Bond world as created by Ian Fleming in his third novel, took place over five days in the early 1950s. They involved Bond trying to stop Sir Hugo Drax from destroying London with a nuclear weapon. But the events of *Moonraker*, as the movie laid them out in 1979, took place only yesterday: There were astronauts; there was the midair theft of a space shuttle; there was Moore happily tumbling around in space with Holly Goodhead (Texas-born actress Lois Chiles, who played an interesting evolution of the Bond Girl—an astronaut and CIA agent; as Chiles put it: "Bond's concession to women's lib"). *Moonraker* would prove an almost equivalent hit to *The Spy Who Loved Me*, and rather surprisingly in the late 1970s, the Bond series, with middle-aged Moore steering the spaceship, was on a middle-aged roll.

TOP SECRET

☛ **CERTAINLY IN THE CASTING** of the savvy (and lovely) Chiles as Holly Goodhead, there was a reach back to the Honor Blackman/Pussy Galore–style Bond Girl. "There is an equal type of thing between Bond and myself," Chiles told *People* magazine. "I'm not a sex kitten." Maybe not, but that name was without doubt the most provocative since Pussy's, was it not? "I thought it a kind of compliment," Chiles said jokingly. "I think my parents thought it meant I was smart."

☛ **WHO IN THE WORLD** are Leila Shenna and Jean-Pierre Castaldi, besides being the two people in the left half of this photograph? They are the actors who portrayed evildoers who gave our hero trouble on an airplane. Shenna, a Moroccan actress turned Bond Girl, had one line in the film: "Any higher, Mr. Bond, and I'm afraid my ears will pop." Castaldi, from France, had earlier been in *The French Connection II*. They stand in here for the hundreds of Bond actors and extras who simply passed through.

☛ **CUBBY BROCCOLI** was the sole producer of the film. He had been impressed by George Lucas's 1977 *Star Wars* and particularly its box office superpower, so he urged that *Moonraker* become as spacey as possible. The novelization of the far-out screenplay, *James Bond and Moonraker*, became a second literary (ahem) best-seller, after Fleming's original.

BOX OFFICE

CRUISE CONTROL. Who, exactly, James Bond was appealing to in the disco/club-hopping/bad-hair latter half of the 1970s does not matter. What does: He was appealing to a lot of people. *Moonraker* sold a fifth again as many tickets in the U.S. as had *The Spy Who Loved Me*, and it made nearly as much money as that film worldwide. If *Goldfinger* was a loud grand slam, these two movies were solid back-to-back doubles, equivalent to *From Russia with Love*, *Diamonds Are Forever* or *Live and Let Die*.

WHAT WOULD FLEMING THINK?

HE PROBABLY WOULD APPLAUD. He was always a modernist, forcing Bond to deal with the latest twists in the Cold War or life in the wider world. In his *Moonraker*, the concerns of British society were the V-2 rocket, a reemergence in England of fascism and particularly a romance with communism, not to mention the so-called "threat from within," accentuated by the activities of turncoat spies like his former MI colleagues Kim Philby and Anthony Blunt. If movie-makers two generations on had his James Bond fighting it out in zero gravity, well, he might have written that himself.

WHAT WOULD FLEMING THINK?

HE MIGHT BE AMAZED. The book *For Your Eyes Only* wasn't really an entity in his eyes: A bunch of half-baked TV scripts that were never produced, that were then turned into stories, that were then collected, that were then dispersed to the movies as bits and pieces of plots and cool titles—"From a View to a Kill," "For Your Eyes Only," "Quantum of Solace" and so forth. Elements of the story "The Hildebrand Rarity" were used in *Licence to Kill,* and it can be said that cloned cells from this book contributed as much to latter-day Bond films as those from any other. So: an afterthought by Fleming, with an enduring afterlife.

FOR YOUR EYES ONLY

As the 1980s dawned, the filmmakers felt it was time for another tweaking—specifically, that the recent films had gotten a bit too out there and needed to come back to earth. "We had gone as far as we could into space," said director John Glen. "We needed a change of some sort, back to the grass roots of Bond. We wanted to make the new film more of a thriller than a romp, without losing sight of what made Bond famous—its humor." To that end, the filmmakers cobbled together a script, a script that underwent regular revisions by committee, from various Ian Fleming writings: two Bond short stories ("For Your Eyes Only" and "Risico"), plus unused bits from novels, including *Goldfinger* (the Identigraph) and *Live and Let Die* (the keel-hauling sequence). There's a hidden missile-command system; episodes in Italy, Greece and England; undersea scenes shot in the Bahamas; a soupçon of Cold War tension for old times' sake. Rather amazingly, it all worked okay as a film, and in 1981 the series celebrated another success. One conspicuous absence: The actor Bernard Lee had died, and rather than immediately replace him as M, a surrogate gave Bond his marching orders.

BOX OFFICE

MONEY IN THE BANK. *For Your Eyes Only* sold 22.4 million tickets in the U.S. and earned nearly $200 million (nearly $500 million today) in the world market. This was the kind of performance Eon Productions was pleased with. There wasn't going to be another *Thunderball,* but if films that could be termed "routine blockbusters" could be churned out, everyone got a raise, and the franchise rolled on.

TOP SECRET

☛ **WHO WAS RICHARD MAIBAUM?** Here, in this conflation of various Fleming short stories, it is time to pay him some attention. He was a screenwriter and producer (*The Big Clock, The Great Gatsby*), born in New York City in 1909. Through his association with Cubby Broccoli in the 1950s, he came to be assigned to the *Dr. No* project, and went on to script or coscript all but three of the Eon Productions Bond films between 1962 and 1989 (he died in 1991). Praise him or blame him, he had something to do with all those stunts, all those wisecracks, all those seduction lines that never would have worked in real life.

☛ **WHO IS CAROLE BOUQUET?** She is a French actress of considerable renown in Europe and, along with Diana Rigg, a Bond Girl of accomplishment to equal her beauty. In 1977 she gained note in Luis Buñuel's *That Obscure Object of Desire,* and on the other side of her Bond experience she won the César Award for best actress for *Too Beautiful for You* (1989). In between, there was the role of Melina Havelock in 1981's *For Your Eyes Only,* and Bond fans remember her only for that. In these two photographs, she is on the set with her costar Roger Moore— as lovely on a gray day as when sparkling in the sun.

☛ **WHO IS JOHN GLEN?** He is an English film director who in 1981 had been a veteran film editor and second-unit director on three Bond films and was about to assume the top job, which he would retain for all five "official" Bond films made in the 1980s—setting the record for most Bond films directed. (Legal entanglements after *Licence to Kill* in 1989 would force an unprecedented six-year hiatus in the series.)

EVERETT

OCTOPUSSY

"**Y**ou don't expect to see Octopussy walking down the aisle at your local supermarket," Maud Adams told *People* magazine back in 1983, adding that she "was quite shocked" when told the title of the next Bond opus, for which she was being recruited. The former model overcame her alarm, signed on the dotted line and thus made history: She would be the first two-time Bond Girl (as opposed to two-timing Bond Girl, of which there had been a few). The provocative title of the movie did in fact originate with Ian Fleming: It had been attached to a short story published posthumously. The source material from the page provided backstory for Adams's title character in the film: empress of a business conglomerate whose name was inspired by Fleming's own pet mollusk. In the ensuing action she assists Bond as he foils a communist plot to nuke West Germany. "Not going to win me any acting merits," admitted Adams, who was 37 when the film was released to much critical smirking. By then, the Bond team was thoroughly inured to smirking.

YEAR OF THE SHOWDOWN

THE ANNUAL SLOGAN on posters in the toddling years of the franchise was: "James Bond Is Back." In the early '80s the phrase whispered with a hiss in the hallways of Eon Productions was: "Sean Connery is back." There might have been an epithet applied before "Sean." Bond fans, for their part, could not have asked for more. Here's what had happened: Kevin McClory had always retained the rights to his *Thunderball* elements and plotlines even after "coming inside" to make that hugely successful film in 1965. Now he, with Connery starring for an exorbitant fee ($5 million, plus a percentage), was going to use those elements and plotlines for a film that would certainly compete with whatever offering Cubby Broccoli sent to the theaters in '83. This created many Fleming-quality subplots, chief among them: Would this be a Moore-Connery face-off? Roger Moore's contract had been up after *Moonraker* and he had agreed to stay on for *For Your Eyes Only*. He was disinclined to make a sixth Bond film, and the name Timothy Dalton was floated as a replacement. James Brolin made three screen tests as Bond during *Octopussy* preps (they live on today in DVD). Finally, though, it was decided the movie needed the tried-and-true if it were to face down the imposing, congenitally rebellious Scotsman. The usually agreeable Moore was approached again, and he accepted the challenge. The bout was set. When the bell rang, *Octopussy* stepped first into the ring, and as if to give royal sanction to the "official" film, the world premiere at the Odeon Leicester Square in London on June 6, 1983, was attended by none other than Prince Charles and Princess Diana (above). Buckingham Palace seemed to have a rooting, if not a betting, interest. Down the road, equably, it would see fit to elevate both Roger and Sean to "Sir."

BOX OFFICE

WINNER BY DECISION.
Octopussy did not dust Sean Connery's *Never Say Never Again* in 1983, but it did come out modestly (if that word can ever be used in a James Bond book) on top. It performed barely less well than had *For Your Eyes Only* (nearly as many tickets sold in the U.S. market). Most important to Cubby Broccoli: It had won the fight, if not by knockout, then by a clear decision. A win was a win.

▰ **VIJAY AMRITRAJ** was a very fine Indian tennis player—a tour champion with 16 titles, he beat Jimmy Connors five times and also John McEnroe—and a very handsome man. Amritraj not only performed in those screen tests opposite Brolin, but played a Bond ally opposite Moore in the film. His movie career never quite panned out, but he remains a hero in his homeland, where he is famous as a philanthropist and activist.

▰ **BRITISH ACTOR ROBERT BROWN** had already appeared in a Bond movie, *The Spy Who Loved Me,* as Admiral Hargreaves. Now, after the producers rested the role of M for one movie out of respect for the late Bernard Lee, Brown began a run as the MI6 chief that would last until 1989. So he is the answer to the question: Who played M in between Bernard Lee and Dame Judi Dench (discounting for a moment Edward Fox, who played the role in the "unofficial" film we discuss on the following page)?

▰ **IT WAS NEVER** made precisely clear whether Brown's character was the same M that had been played by Lee or an entirely new boss. Incidentally: The role of Q, as still portrayed by actor Desmond Llewelyn, was expanded.

☞ **KEVIN MCCLORY** has popped up more than once in our book, always as part of the *Thunderball* plotline. Who was he, beyond a collaborator on a script with Ian Fleming that won him a lifetime of legal rights to play around with Bond, Blofeld and company? He was a handsome Irish World War II veteran (when his ship was torpedoed, he spent two weeks in a lifeboat in the North Atlantic) who, postwar, involved himself in the production side of movies and was once romantically involved with Elizabeth Taylor. Before all their many court appearances, he was Ian Fleming's close friend. Even after the profitable satisfaction of making *Thunderball* and then *Never Say Never Again*, he kept trying to spin his slice of Bond, but *Warhead 2000 A.D.* never came to pass. He died at age 80 in 2006.

☞ **THE GREAT MAX VON SYDOW,** who made 13 films with Ingmar Bergman during his career, portrayed Blofeld here, and certainly the role of this evil genius is the most richly and variously portrayed in BondWorld—besides, perhaps, that of 007 himself. Oddly, in von Sydow's interpretation, Blofeld kept the white cat, even though this was an affectation created for the earlier Eon films and not by Fleming.

NEVER SAY NEVER AGAIN

Most of the lawsuits were between Ian Fleming and Kevin McClory, and the upshot was: McClory still, even after negotiating his participation in *Thunderball* and seeing that film made—and become the most lucrative of all Bond movies—retained the rights to have his own vision of Bond return to the screen in the future. After making *Diamonds Are Forever*, Sean Connery had emphatically said he would "never again" play Bond, but money talks, and so the most famous of all 007s returned to battle against Blofeld, and now against Cubby Broccoli and Co. as well. Even the toupee was streaked in gray this time out, and Connery, as ever, had good sport with his character's conceits and foibles. The movie was fine—it was better received, critically, than *Octopussy*—and Connery's fans were glad to see him again. But they were also willing to bid him, 52 when he shot the film, a final adieu, for as Roger Moore, too, was learning at age 56: The world had little need for an old James Bond.

BOX OFFICE

RUNNER-UP. As mentioned in our assessment of *Octopussy*, *Never Say Never Again* was slightly less profitable. But a few points to note: Both movies made plenty of money; together they made nearly three-quarters of a billion in adjusted (2012) dollars. And interestingly, while *Octopussy* earned more worldwide, *Never Say Never Again* had only a marginally lower take in the U.S., where, perhaps, the idea that Connery *was* Bond remained stronger.

THE SHOWDOWN, PART II

THIS OF COURSE would not be just about Connery versus Moore, it would be about competing M's and Q's, which plot was better and, not least, a battle of the Bond Girls. The *Octopussy* production tried to proceed carefully, just as it had in entreating Moore to return. Sybil Danning was considered as the title character, as was Barbara Carrera, who actually claimed to have turned down the part to become what would turn out to be the competing *Never Say Never Again*'s Bond Girl No. 2. Finally Cubby Broccoli decided Maud Adams would return to the Eon series, hair darkened so she wouldn't look precisely like the other Bond Girl she had recently played. Over in *Never* land, Sean Connery's wife, Micheline, had become acquainted with the 29-year-old American actress Kim Basinger (opposite) and suggested she might be right as Domino. Connery concurred, and the producers were quickly concurring with just about everything he was concurring with. Basinger, like Adams a former model, went on to portray a second memorable "girl" role as *Batman*'s Vicki Vale, then to a distinguished career that included a Best Actress Oscar for *L.A. Confidential*. A footnote: Also in *Never Say Never Again*, in a small role, was the British comedian Rowan Atkinson, who would later skewer Bond deftly in *Johnny English*.

BOND-WORTHY VILLAINS

THE SINGULAR recording artist and club queen Grace Jones, seen here, made for the best pictures, but, as May Day, girlfriend and henchwoman of the evil Max Zorin, she was only the second most impressive Bond nemesis in *A View to a Kill*. Zorin was played by Christopher Walken, and his over-the-top malevolence was, many thought, the best thing in the film. (Roger Moore didn't agree, as is explained on the opposite page.) Also on board against Bond (for the first time) was real-world Jones boyfriend Dolph Lundgren as a KGB bodyguard. He had been visiting Jones on the set one day, and director John Glen gave him a job.

A VIEW TO A KILL

Suddenly, there was something about Roger Moore's looks. Sean Connery saw it: "Bond should be played by an actor 35, 33 years old. I'm too old. Roger's too old, too!" In 2007, long after the film had had its run and Moore had retired from the role, Moore good-naturedly avowed, "I was only about 400 years too old for the part [in *A View to a Kill*]." But that wasn't the only reason he was walking out of MI6 headquarters for the last time: "I was horrified on the last Bond I did. Whole slews of sequences where Christopher Walken was machine-gunning hundreds of people. I said, 'That wasn't Bond, those aren't Bond films.' It stopped being what they were all about. You didn't dwell on the blood and the brains spewing all over the place." But it was now 1985, and the films, which had always piled on the jokes and gadgets, were piling on in other ways. If they had left Connery and Moore behind—finally, after 23 years of movies—well, then they had left Sean and Roger behind.

TOP SECRET

☛ **THE CASTING OF GRACE JONES** would have pleased Ian Fleming: She hailed from his beloved Jamaica. She started her career as a model and, taken under the wing of none other than Andy Warhol, she became a fixture at New York City's Studio 54 during the disco era. She had a bunch of dance-club hits—representative: "Pull Up to the Bumper"— then started her acting career, playing to type since, really, looking as she did, she had no option.

☛ **THE MOVIE STARRED** one hitmaker in Jones, and almost starred two: David Bowie was sought for the role of Zorin, and Sting was discussed, before Christopher Walken took the part and made it his.

☛ **THIS WAS THE 14TH** and last Bond film to feature Lois Maxwell as Miss Moneypenny. Along the way she had also appeared in the TV series *The Saint* and *Danger Man* (in the U.S., called *Secret Agent*) and in the Bond spoof *OK Connery* (in the U.S., *Operation Kid Brother*).

BOX OFFICE

HOLDING PATTERN. The film, generally derided by the critics, performed ably with the public: just over 14 million tickets sold in the U.S., another worldwide take of more than $150 million ($325 million when adjusted for inflation)—reflective of the steady-as-she-goes success of the franchise for most of the 1980s. Now we would see if that could be maintained in the post-Moore era.

THE LIVING DAYLIGHTS

Everyone knew Roger Moore was done, and for a short time everyone seemed to know Pierce Brosnan would replace him. *People* magazine said as much. But then—thanks to all the publicity "the next Bond" was getting—Brosnan's TV series, *Remington Steele*, was renewed for another season; Brosnan was contractually committed to continue; and Cubby Broccoli said, "Remington Steele will not be James Bond." Brosnan lamented: "Certain things in life are meant to happen— this obviously wasn't one of them." The tall, handsome, classically trained Welshman Timothy Dalton, who had felt he was too young to play Bond when considered for *On Her Majesty's Secret Service*, was signed in his stead. When *People* asked for an interview in 1987, Dalton's representatives demanded a four-page cover story "like you gave Pierce Brosnan." *People*'s editors declined. Perhaps they knew something. Dalton's tenure as Bond would be short-lived—two movies—and controversial, as the series took a turn toward the somber that, while appreciated by certain critics (*The Washington Post* felt *The Living Daylights* was the best Bond ever), quickly seemed to fall flat with the public. The public, Cubby Broccoli always realized, was paying the bills.

WAIT AND SEE.
The Living Daylights performed admirably if not spectacularly. It was up in worldwide gross over Moore's swan song, and it sold only about a million fewer tickets in the U.S. The critics were happy, Cubby Broccoli was happy enough. Timothy Dalton would be back.

TOP SECRET

☞ **DESMOND LLEWELYN,** seen at right with Timothy Dalton (left), was the last of MI6's Big Three, along with Bernard Lee as M and Lois Maxwell as Moneypenny, to still be persevering with the franchise. A Welshman like Dalton, Llewelyn had been a second lieutenant in the British army when captured by the Germans during World War II; he spent five years as a prisoner of war. Terence Young had worked with him in the 1950s, and brought him aboard the Bond series in 1963. Llewelyn would make 17 Bond films before being killed in a car accident at age 85 in 1999. Interestingly, the man who will always be, for many of us, Q, was not tech savvy—nor was his successor as MI6 gadgeteer, the Monty Python alum and comic actor John Cleese.

☞ **IN BETWEEN HIS TWO BOND FILMS,** Dalton hastened back to the London stage and starred opposite Vanessa Redgrave in Eugene O'Neill's *A Touch of the Poet,* for which he (and she) received strong reviews. Redgrave was Dalton's companion from 1980 to 1994.

☞ **DALTON RETURNED BOND TO THE CIGARETTES** that had been Bond's (and Fleming's) habit. But his would be the last smoking Bond. As for martinis, Dalton said later, "I don't think I've drunk one since I've left the Bond movies."

WHAT WOULD FLEMING THINK?

HE WOULD BE THRILLED. After years of seeing filmmakers ignore his written word in devising their plots, he would be pleased that the beginning of *The Living Daylights* follows the plot of his short story of the same name, in which Bond seeks to protect a Soviet defector. Moreover, he would be happy with the tack toward the more serious, grittier Bond of the page. Lastly, considering all from the vantage of today, he would note that *The Living Daylights* was the last film until the Daniel Craig era began in 2006 to even bother using one of his story or novel titles as the name of the movie.

TOP SECRET

 **THE WORKING TITLE** of the screenplay, a script that would have precious little to do with Ian Fleming source material, was *Licence Revoked,* because a major plot development was to be the suspension of Bond's famous 00 license to kill. Perhaps sensing, correctly, that this wasn't what fans needed to hear, the film's title was altered, but the plot twist was retained.

 **CAREY LOWELL,** seen here with Dalton and opposite with him and Llewelyn, was the latest of the new generation of intelligent, formidable (but still lovely) Bond Girls. The actress was also known for taking her turn as an intelligent, formidable and lovely assistant district attorney in TV's *Law & Order.*

 **BUDGETARY AND TAX** reasons mandated that *Licence to Kill* was the first Bond film not filmed at the famous Pinewood Studios outside London, which had been up and running since the 1930s and, in film circles, synonymous with the Bond franchise since the '60s.

LICENCE TO KILL

In 1989 the critics, as if finally hearing the murmurs of many longtime Bond fans—murmurs that had begun the very day *The Living Daylights* had opened two years earlier—started to question the rightness of Timothy Dalton in the role. Some twigged to the fact that, as Richard Corliss put it in his essay earlier in our book, the theater guy "seemed to be performing under protest." Gritty and authentic are good; dour is not. There were lively enough costars working the bad-guy side of the aisle in *Licence to Kill*—a young Benicio Del Toro! a not-young Wayne Newton!—but they weren't able to sufficiently enliven the proceedings. The release and reception of *Licence to Kill* brought the movie franchise to one of those occasional moments of truth: Was Bond, at long last, toast? In a blessing of sorts, legal squabbles forced the moviemakers to take time off, and it would be more than six years before 007 reappeared on the big screen. By the time he did, he had a new face. And a new energy.

KEITH HAMSHERE/MGM/MPTVIMAGES

BOX OFFICE

BLAH. The producers pointed out that the film was profitable, and that it had faced stiff competition in the 1989 marketplace from *Batman, Lethal Weapon 2* and *Indiana Jones and the Last Crusade* (costarring Sean Connery—curse him!). But the film was off nearly $100 million (adjusted) worldwide from *The Living Daylights,* and it sold fewer than 10 million tickets in the U.S.—the first time any Bond film had done that. American audiences, in particular, hadn't warmed to Timothy Dalton.

MGM/MPTVIMAGES

GOLDENEYE

Critics and fans alike were prepared to pronounce it D.O.A. The Bond series had been gone so long that many thought it was gone for good. The start of *GoldenEye*, even after the legal hurdles were cleared, was so often delayed that Timothy Dalton simply informed producers he was quitting. When Pierce Brosnan was finally signed, there was little of the buzz that had attended his near-signing nine years earlier. Barbara Broccoli, not her legendary father, was now in charge. The Berlin Wall had fallen, leaving Bond without one of his raisons d'être. There was so much going against this film . . . but then: There were so many smart decisions—or at least half-decisions—made. The real-world MI6 in London had named a woman chief, and so the film brought on the great Judi Dench as M. Bono and the Edge were brought in to write the theme song. Sean Bean (below, with Brosnan, as an MI6 colleague who would soon go bad) proved an intriguing villain. Bond truly was back, for the first time in a long while.

WHAT WOULD FLEMING THINK?

HE MIGHT HAVE BEEN FLATTERED. This was the first Bond film with zero story or title elements from the author. "GoldenEye" was merely a tribute nod to Fleming's Jamaican estate and perhaps to that World War II mission he had been involved in. But Fleming was a vain man, and perhaps that alone would have assuaged him.

TOP SECRET

☞ **JUDI DENCH,** it is now clear, is the one person who could have been cast as precisely the right M for both the Brosnan years and the Craig era. So talented is she, she can play wry, smart, tough, funny—whatever is asked. She quickly sized up agent 007, as personified by Brosnan, as a "sexist, misogynist dinosaur," and the audience smiled. Finally: a gag worth smiling at! Besides her Bond work, which has continued since 1995, she has won an Oscar for Best Supporting Actress, a Tony for Best Actress and been named Dame Commander of the Order of the British Empire.

☞ **FAMKE JANSSEN,** a Dutch A-list fashion model, cut a ferocious figure as the villain Xenia Onatopp, seen here in close contact with Brosnan's Bond. She, in different ways than Judi Dench, was not destined to be remembered exclusively (or even best) for her Bond affiliation. As Jean Grey/Phoenix in the *X-Men* movies, she is a living legend among teenage boys.

☞ **SEAN BEAN** is a third member of the supporting cast of *GoldenEye* who has bucked the trend of being defined by his Bondness. He was, indeed, memorable as Alec Trevelyan—MI6 agent 006 left for dead, who really wasn't, and who rose to oppose 007 with an international crime organization. But no one would claim this British actor is better remembered as Trevelyan than he is as Boromir in the *Lord of the Rings* trilogy, which in the years subsequent to *GoldenEye* made James Bond look like a nice, successful enough little film series.

TOMORROW NEVER DIES

Many things had come full circle since the Bond series's heyday in the 1960s. Consider, for just a moment, how different Bond and the Beatles seemed back then, a point made earlier in our book. And now here we are with the title of a Bond film being inspired by a Beatles song ("Tomorrow Never Knows," from the *Revolver* album). With no Fleming novels left to adapt, and not even worried about using Fleming titles anymore, the writers were playing with the Lennon-McCartney phrase and when the folks at MGM saw the variation "Tomorrow Never Dies," they said: That's it. So there it is, a Bond-Beatles rapprochement after all these years. Other things were different, too. Cubby Broccoli had died before this 1997 release was made, and so Bond would have to soldier on without even his blessing. Perhaps ominously, this became the first Brosnan Bond to not open at No. 1 in the U.S., debuting as it did on the same day as *Titanic*. But for all the change, everything came out well enough—and it was clear that, for Bond, the final end was not yet in sight.

BOX OFFICE

JUST FINE. The Brosnan years were remarkably consistent in terms of both artistic achievement and performance at the ticket booth: In neither realm was there anything earth-shaking, but there were no disappointments. *Tomorrow Never Dies* did a little better in America than *GoldenEye* had, and a touch worse worldwide. But still, an adjusted gross of $479,400,000 indicated great strength for the franchise.

TOP SECRET

☞ **THE PRINCIPAL VILLAIN** in the movie, played with pizzazz by Jonathan Pryce, is Elliot Carver, a media mogul bent on world domination—he's hoping to start a global war to make it easier to obtain exclusive broadcasting rights in Asia—and if that sounds like Rupert Murdoch, it shouldn't. The character was said to be modeled on Murdoch's late, great rival, Robert Maxwell.

☞ **ALSO ON THE VILLAIN FRONT,** it is quite possible that the actor Götz Otto, Pryce's henchman and chief agent of torture (he prefers the Chakra method), delivered the shortest audition in the long history of Bond films. Given 20 seconds to convince the filmmakers he should be cast, he took five: "I am big, I am bad and I am German."

☞ **LASTLY ON THE VILLAIN FRONT:** Actress Sela Ward, then pushing 40, auditioned to play Pryce's wife, but in the brutal way of the Bond world—and Hollywood in general— was reportedly told she was fine but needed to be 10 years younger. She couldn't pull that off, and 32-year-old Teri Hatcher got the role. Ward's small consolation: Hatcher said later, "It's such an artificial kind of character to be playing that you don't get any special satisfaction from it."

UNITED ARTISTS/EVERETT

KEITH HAMSHERE © 1997 MGM/UA/MPTVIMAGES

CLASS ACT

MICHELLE YEOH, the preternaturally beautiful Malaysian actress, was cast as Colonel Wai Lin, a Chinese spy whose martial arts expertise makes the term *Bond Girl* seem foolish; Brosnan himself said it was better to think of her as a "female James Bond." Yeoh did most of her own stunts in the film, and she would gain worldwide renown for her prowess later in the 2000 film *Crouching Tiger, Hidden Dragon.* She would later still be deported from Burma after portraying the pro-democracy leader Aung San Suu Kyi in *The Lady.*

☞ **MICHAEL APTED** is among the most interesting choices as director in the history of Bond. A noted documentarian (the *Up* series) and a bit of a legend in England, with a strong reputation for working with women (Sissy Spacek won the Oscar for *Coal Miner's Daughter* and Sigourney Weaver and Jodie Foster have been nominated for their work in Apted films), Apted stands out as particularly artsy in the roster of Bond helmsmen. But when all was said and done, he made a Bond film.

☞ **PETER JACKSON,** a big Bond fan since his boyhood in New Zealand, had been considered as director. Barbara Broccoli had been impressed by his feature *Heavenly Creatures* starring the rookie Kate Winslet. In the end, Apted was signed—and after Jackson made his *Lord of the Rings* trilogy he said he doubted he would get another shot at Bond anytime soon, since the series rarely employed celebrity directors.

☞ **JOE DANTE,** the American director of *Gremlins*, was another interesting candidate for this project, and a further indication that the series' new bosses were willing to think outside the box—an attitude that would be reflected in the choice of Sam Mendes for 2012's *Skyfall*.

THE WORLD IS NOT ENOUGH

The plot, assembled by three credited screenwriters, involved the assassination of a British oil billionaire by a former KGB agent–turned-terrorist and Bond's effort to protect the billionaire's daughter, Elektra King (played by Sophie Marceau, opposite), who had earlier been kidnapped but escaped, and the subsequent discovery by Bond that there existed a plan to inflate petroleum prices with a nuclear meltdown off Istanbul, and Elektra was probably involved, and . . . The plot, as we were beginning to say, was so convoluted that Pierce Brosnan himself admitted to being confused. But such trivial problems never kept a Bond film from being made in the past, and they wouldn't now. Maybe all would become clear in the record-breaking roughly-14-minute prelude sequence that fronted the film before credits rolled. Then again, maybe not. It hardly mattered. By now, Bond and Brosnan fans knew what to expect, and that was the familiar formula, slickly delivered: cool vehicles, egregious jokes, psychotic bad guys. It really was time, however, with the millennium drawing to a close, to wonder anew how much longer the producers could get away with this.

CLASS ACTS

WAS Q QUITTING? It seemed he might be when the MI6 quartermaster, played for the 17th time by Desmond Llewelyn, introduced Bond to a somewhat younger man he was training, played by John Cleese. "If you're Q," asked Bond, "does that make him R?" The question is never answered, but Llewelyn was killed in the aforementioned automobile accident shortly after wrapping the film, and Cleese played the Q—or R—role in the final Brosnan film.

BOX OFFICE

BROSNANESQUE. *The World Is Not Enough*'s performance was the mirror image of that of *Tomorrow Never Dies:* maybe a touch worse in the U.S. market, a touch better overall with an adjusted worldwide gross of just under a half billion ($498,390,000). Such boring, predictable accounting does nothing but make moviemakers smile.

BOX OFFICE

BOFFO. Ironies abound in this being Pierce Brosnan's last Bond film. It was his biggest hit of the four. In terms of pure dollars ($431,933,000), it was the highest grossing Bond film to date, and even when adjusted for inflation was in the series' top 10 with $550,970,000. There certainly were discussions about bringing Brosnan back, and he was keen, but finally the producers had the nerve to seek a thorough reboot of the series, and thus ended all plotlines already established in the franchise.

DIE ANOTHER DAY

In a way, the viewing audience said goodbye a decade ago to a Bond it had long known and loved. Yes, yes: This year's celebration is of a half century of Bond, but the Sean Connery–Terence Young template of a suave, devilish, wisecracking superspy was used for the last time in 2002's *Die Another Day.* George Lazenby, Roger Moore, Timothy Dalton and Pierce Brosnan each put his individual spin on the character, but for 40 years there were rules that couldn't be broken. Now (some would add, finally) the producers themselves felt a new direction was necessary. They certainly must have been influenced by *The Bourne Identity* starring Matt Damon, released the same year as *Die Another Day.* Had the two films been booked on a double bill, the Bond would have looked like a cartoon lead-in. So the producers wanted some of that kind of action, and a whole new kind of Bond. Whether they could pull it off was yet to be seen. First, the fans of the old Bond gave 007 a grand send-off by thronging to the multiplexes for *Die Another Day.*

KEITH HAMSHERE © 2002 MGM/MPTVIMAGES

MGM/EVERETT

NEW TOYS

CGI TECHNOLOGY BECAME THE THING, and so of course it became a Bond thing. Too much so? Director Lee Tamahori (above, with Brosnan) played with it in *Die Another Day.* Excessively, said some critics. One of the boo-birds was none other than Roger Moore: "I thought it just went too far—and that's from me, the first Bond in space! Invisible cars and dodgy CGI footage? Please!"

CLASS ACTS

IN *DIE ANOTHER DAY* a true Hollywood superstar and former beauty queen, Halle Berry (opposite), appeared as the principal Bond Girl, Jinx Johnson. In 2001, the year before *Die Another Day* was released, Berry had appeared in *Monster's Ball,* for which she won the Best Actress Oscar. (She remains, to date, the only African American woman so honored.) She acquitted herself as Jinx, if not as Catwoman, for which she was given, in 2005, the Golden Raspberry Award for Worst Actress. Class act that she is, she showed up in person to accept. Also showing at a gala, below, was Queen Elizabeth II, who attended the world premiere of *Die Another Day* at London's Royal Albert Hall on November 18, 2002. The queen's history with Bond was hardly finished, as she would be memorably accompanied by her Secret Service agent to the Olympics Opening Ceremonies in July of 2012.

CAMERA PRESS/ROTA/REDUX

KEITH HAMSHERE/UNITED ARTISTS

TOP SECRET

➤ **A PG-13 RATING** was, the Bond producers knew, essential for the film to bring in a wide enough audience to perform to expectations in the American market, and this rating was in jeopardy due to steamy sex scenes between Bond and Bond Girls. The footage was reedited, and the toned-down version passed muster.

➤ **THE TITLE SONG** for the film was sung by Madonna. She is, of course, a woman of many talents, and so appeared in the film as well: in a small part, as Verity, a fencing instructor to Gustav Graves, the main bad guy.

➤ **ONE RECORD SET** by the production was of dubious distinction: Most Money Received in Return for Product Placements. Reportedly, as many as 24 companies paid some $100 million or even more to have their goods featured in the film. In articles on the mini-scandal, more than one media outlet opted for the obvious Bondian pun: "Buy Another Day."

CLASS ACTS

ONE ACTOR ONLY was carried over from Bond's prior cinematic history: Dame Judi Dench as M. She's the same character, but different playing opposite Daniel Craig than she was with Pierce Brosnan. She no longer gets in an amiable huff about Bond's macho tendencies but, rather, tries to help him grow in a difficult and dangerous profession. Craig, of course, has art-house movies in his past (as well as Hollywood fare, to be sure), and photographs like the one on this page, with these two actors, could just as easily have been taken on a *Masterpiece Theatre* set as on that of a Bond film.

CASINO ROYALE [PART III]

This was the grand experiment, with much more of a commitment made than when Timothy Dalton had been hired. The Dalton episode represented, maybe, a big tweak. This was an overhaul, a reinvention. If the Bond film series was to reach its 50th anniversary 10 years hence, everything rested on this vigorous left turn in direction. Everything rested, as well, on the strong shoulders of Daniel Craig, a no-nonsense English actor who had gained notice on the telly, in smaller British films and then big-budget Hollywood offerings such as *Lara Croft: Tomb Raider*. When Craig had agreed to play Bond, there was a general understanding that Bond was heading in somewhat new directions, but he realized as well that the living ghost of Sean Connery was out there; that sex was still part of the deal and if he was asked to pull an Ursula Andress or Halle Berry and stride meaningfully from the surf, then he was to do so; and if he had a hit on his hands, he would return. All good in 2006, and all still good six years later as Craig's third Bond outing, *Skyfall*, is about to open in the year of Bond's jubilee.

WHAT WOULD FLEMING THINK?

HE WOULD SAY, "FINALLY!" He would say, "I don't care if he didn't go to Eton! That's my boy!" He would say, "Okay, now let's do the 12 novels over again. In order. Next up is *Live and Let Die*, then we do *Moonraker*, then . . ." He would know, immediately, that Daniel Craig had done his homework, reading all the books the moment he agreed to take on the role. If Fleming had any qualm at all, it might be that a high-stakes poker game was substituted for his novel's baccarat. Fleming deftly taught his readers the rules of baccarat before posing Bond and Le Chiffre to have at it, and his set piece is masterfully conceived and executed. Surely the film producers figured that more folks in the moviegoing audience understood poker, what with ESPN televising the World Series from Vegas each year, and chose the simpler route. Probably a sound decision, as Fleming would agree.

JAY MAIDMENT/© 2006 MGM/PHOTO BY MPTVIMAGES (2)

BOND-WORTHY VILLAINS

PETER LORRE AND ORSON WELLES had both played Le Chiffre in earlier *Casino Royale*s, but not they nor anyone else, Gert Fröbe and Götz Otto included, ever brought a better stage name to the Bond Bad Guy Roll of Dishonor than the third actor to take on the card-player's role: Mads Mikkelsen. The Danish actor was, as a bonus, terrific, and later his talent was confirmed with the 2012 Best Actor award at Cannes for his role in *The Hunt*. Also fine in *Casino Royale* was Caterina Murino, whose dark, conflicted character Solange is seduced by Bond (below), then murdered by Le Chiffre.

JAY MAIDMENT/COLUMBIA PICTURES

TOP SECRET

☛ **BARBARA BROCCOLI** and her colleagues would never want this to get around, but the 2006 version of *Casino Royale* has more in common with the 1954 television adaptation of *Casino Royale* than it does with most if not all of the other films in Eon's 50-year Bond series. In 1954 the TV folk were trying to bring Fleming's character and plot to the screen, and that was the purist goal in 2006 as well.

☛ **REBOOTS DO NOT** have technical requirements, but essentially what "reboot" means is: a new telling independent of what you might have seen before. So Bond is fresh to the 00 game here—in fact, at the film's beginning he doesn't yet have his license to kill—and exhibits some of the doubts and insecurities of Fleming's younger Bond. More concretely, various things go missing in a reboot, including, here, the character of Miss Moneypenny, who had worked at MI6 in every film since 1962.

☛ **NOT ONLY CHARLIZE THERON** but Angelina Jolie was considered for the role of Vesper Lynd, which eventually went to Eva Green, who was fine indeed. Jolie, in particular, might have tipped the focus away from the crucial question at hand: How was the film itself?

☞ **PAUL HAGGIS** cowrote the screenplays for both *Casino Royale* and *Quantum of Solace*. He also produced and wrote *Million Dollar Baby*, which starred and was directed by Clint Eastwood and which was named Best Picture for 2004. Haggis followed that up with *Crash*, which he wrote and directed, and for which he won Oscars in the Best Picture and Best Writing categories—becoming the first person ever to script two Best Picture winners in a row.

☞ **HAVING SAID THAT ABOUT HAGGIS,** none other that Daniel Craig expressed the opinion that his second Bond film could and should have been better, and less of a direct sequel to *Casino Royale*. He said that a writers' strike left the production with an unfinished scenario.

☞ **TWO OF HAGGIS'S CO-SCENARISTS** on *Quantum* and *Casino* were Neal Purvis and Robert Wade. They also helped script the Brosnan films *Die Another Day* and *The World Is Not Enough*. Fascinatingly, they also worked on the spoof *Johnny English*, starring Rowan Atkinson. Back in Cubby's day, that might have gotten them canned from 007 forever.

QUANTUM OF SOLACE

Michael G. Wilson is certainly a major figure in the recent history of the Bond franchise. He happens to be the stepson of Cubby Broccoli and older half-brother of Barbara Broccoli. Makes sense: The Bond series has long been a family affair dear to the Broccolis, and Cubby was wont to promote from within—writers, directors, even coproducers. Wilson has, in recent years, become a central figure in the rebirth of the franchise, and this film—a huge success—is largely due to him. During the filming of *Casino Royale*, he started thinking about plot extensions (Bond getting revenge for the death of his lover Vesper Lynd, and other things). He essentially drafted *Quantum of Solace*—for which he appropriated the title (but none of the plot) of an early Ian Fleming short story—in his head. Three screenwriters (including Paul Haggis, discussed on the opposite page) who were familiar with both Wilson and also *Royale*, and who were keen on the new direction of Bond, went to work on Wilson's ideas, and the second film of the Craig era was underway.

BOX OFFICE

BOFFO. Everyone who went to see the new *Casino Royale* went to see *Quantum of Solace*—minus maybe a couple of people—and Hollywood had confirmation that the reboot had been brilliantly achieved. Despite the adjusted $624,690,000 take of *Quantum*, MGM had financial woes that would slow the start of *Skyfall* a bit. But Bond would be back, there was no doubt about that, and just in time for his 50th birthday.

CLASS ACT

SOME BOND GIRLS down the decades may have worked as hard as Olga Kurylenko (opposite, with Craig), who played Camille Montes. But none worked harder. She trained for weeks to learn how to handle weapons and do stunts. She watched the previous Bond films and became an admirer of the physical Michelle Yeoh in *Tomorrow Never Dies*. Asked if she was proud of being a Bond Girl, she said she was proud that she did her own tricks.

SKYFALL

Back in the day, Bond filmmakers used to count their pennies. *Quantum of Solace* had a reported budget of more than $200 million. The point is: The franchise is not only 50 years old and happy to be around, it is a player at the highest levels of Hollywood moviemaking and is seeking, like Blofeld might, world domination every time out. And speaking of Blofeld, when *Skyfall* was filming there were all sorts of rumors that he was to return, and that the Ralph Fiennes character that had been disclosed—"Gareth Mallory, a government agent"—was just a cover. Voldemort might play Blofeld? What could be more delicious! All of these "as we go to press"–type things have been good fun to parse in recent days, but what matters is: *He made it.* Commander Bond made it. Fifty-nine years after first appearing on the page, 50 years after hitting the big screen for the first time, only a few weeks after escorting the queen to the Olympics, he is not only still with us, he is buffed, ballistically armed and big budget.

REX FEATURES/AP

FRANCOIS DUHAMEL/SONY/AP

CLASS ACTS

JUDI DENCH not only returns, she has a pivotal role as M becomes the subject of a government investigation after her past comes back to haunt her. In the course of the movie, even Bond, having learned too much about M, wonders about her. Dench and Craig (right) were obviously thrilled to be working with director Sam Mendes (here consulting with Dench). The English stage and film veteran won the directing Oscar for *American Beauty,* worked with Craig on *Road to Perdition* and brought yet more of the recent gilt and gravitas as well as glamour to the Bond franchise. Now we get to see how he did.

TEASING
COMMANDER BOND

Ever since Sean Connery took on the job, Bond has teased himself. "But not enough!" said a hit squad of satirists down through the decades.

On the previous page and on these two, we have three of the elite funnymen of the postwar period: Rowan Atkinson, Mike Myers (opposite) and the late Don Adams (with the shoe phone, connecting with the afterlife). Their intersection in this case is James Bond, and at that address they find a veritable frat house full of fellow comedians. Some of them have impersonated Bondish characters on forgettable *Saturday Night Live* or *That Was the Week That Was* skits (in fact, it was in a pretty lame sketch on a British variety show in 1964—viewable now on YouTube—that Roger Moore first appeared as 007, playing the spy on vacation). But others—including Atkinson, Myers and Adams—have created indelible knockoff personas that will live in celluloid as long as the Bond movies themselves, providing hilarious counterpoint. Bond was never, in the Connery and most other interpretations, a stuffed shirt, but still he was ripe for skewering. Those wielding the skewers have done us a great service.

Just as *The Man from U.N.C.L.E.* was a direct response to the 007 phenomenon of the early 1960s (even unto its direct Ian Fleming association), Don Adams's TV series *Get Smart* was happy to be as blatant as possible that his Agent 86, Maxwell Smart, was all about Bond . . . James Bond. As funny as the ubiquitous shoe phone was, funnier still was the shoe blade that was inserted backwards into Maxwell Smart's footwear, so that when he clicked his heels à la *From Russia with Love*'s Rosa Klebb, he stabbed himself. *Get Smart* was, at the time, wild—truly wild. "I was sick of looking at all those nice sensible situation comedies," cocreator (with Buck Henry) Mel Brooks told *Time* magazine in 1965. "I wanted to do a crazy, unreal comic-strip kind of thing."

Get Smart was so much better than the Bond movie knockoffs—James Coburn's *Flint* films, Dean Martin's Matt Helms—all of which, with one eye cautiously on the box office, could not quite decide whether they wanted to bedevil Bond or *be* Bond. Decades later, when the mania had calmed and imitation would offer no kind of financial success, there was only one option remaining: Be funny or be gone. Myers released the first of his three *Austin Powers* films, subtitled *International Man of Mystery*, in 1997, when no one would have suspected there was much point in satirizing the 1960s or '60s superspies. Of course, this left the field wide open for Powers to cruise cluelessly about in his Shaguar, in a performance that was—crucially—over-the-top. He drew howls from the young (who didn't really get it) and also their parents and even grandparents (who

really, perhaps painfully, did). Myers played the Blofeld character, Dr. Evil, in the series as well, and when you throw in the idea of Mini Me, it all adds up to a kind of psychedelic tour de force.

Atkinson's character Johnny English, who bowed in 2003 and would appear in two movies, was more . . . ummm . . . *subtle*. Here you had a performer who could kill (as they say in comedy) with a look; consider once more, if you will, how earnest he is on the previous page, and yet he's uproarious.

Is there a point to be made? Maybe that James Bond was a target that was precise, but also something of a blank canvas upon which geniuses of various kinds might paint their pictures.

Not all who stepped up, brushes in hand, were geniuses—to be sure. In this chapter we review a host of other send-ups that were far lesser than *Johnny English, Austin Powers* or *Get Smart*, but that elicited a belly laugh or at least a smile with their efforts. *The Flintstones* saw fit to take on Bond, and so did the Beatles. Insiders

EVERETT

like Roger Moore and Sean Connery's little brother felt they had a license to kill the sacred cow. They each took their shot. Some were hits, some were misses.

The most successful of them, it seems clear, proceeded with affection—and that was something crucial to the audience waiting to meet them at their common intersection: James Bond.

NEW LINE CINEMA/PHOTOFEST

ADDER PODS/KOBAL/ART RESOURCE, NY

EVERETT

MONDADORI/EVERETT

MARY EVANS/PRODUZIONE D.S./RONALD GRANT/EVERETT

WORKING TITLE/DAVID APPLEBY/KOBAL/ART RESOURCE, NY

FOUR FROM THE '60s, when the world was goofy; one from later, when goofy ruled the world. Above, clockwise from top left: Scenes from *Carry On Spying,* with Charles Hawtrey, Kenneth Williams, Bernard Cribbins and Barbara Windsor; *Dr. Goldfoot and the Bikini Machine,* starring Dwayne Hickman; *Operation Kid Brother,* starring the real kid brother Neil Connery and former real Bond Girl Daniela Bianchi; and *Kiss the Girls and Make Them Die,* with Margaret Lee scared by a scorpion while Mike Connors (soon to gain fame as Joe Mannix), has the drop on the arachnid. Opposite: Atkinson as Johnny English, boning up. He has given us not only this classic comic character but also Blackadder and Mr. Bean, plus, recently, the second-funniest performance at the Olympics Opening Ceremonies after Daniel Craig's "James Bond."

HANNA-BARBERA/EVERETT

COSGROVE HALL FILMS/EVERETT

EVERETT

MELINDA SUE GORDON/NEW LINE CINEMA

TWENTIETH CENTURY FOX/PHOTOFEST

CARTOONS AND CARTOONISH: Above, clockwise from top left, *The Man Called Flintstone; Danger Mouse;* Roger Moore sending up himself in *The Cannonball Run;* the Beatles on the run in *Help!* Apparently they and their producers had heard that the latest Bond film was to shoot scenes in the Bahamas and they said, "Let's go there." Part of the chase music made for the film involved the use of the exotic Indian instrument the sitar, and George Harrison became intrigued, and, well, yes: The rest is history. Opposite: Scenes from the life of Mike Myers's Austin Powers, clockwise from top in *Goldmember,* then *International Man of Mystery* (with Elizabeth Hurley) and then *The Spy Who Shagged Me* (with Heather Graham). *Groovy, bay-beeee!*

BOND WORLD

They sometimes come into the open, for instance these two Miss Moneypennys, Lois Maxwell and Samantha Bond, at an auction viewing in London. But more often they lurk in the shadows—everywhere on the planet, fellow . . . Bond Nuts. The writer Len Feldman is one. He has Bond memorabilia, tapes, interviews and a keen personal appreciation and encyclopedic knowledge of a film saga that now stretches a half century. LIFE Books asked Len to edify our readers, and challenge his fraternal and sororal Bond Nuts among them. Here, then, a guided tour of BondWorld— Len's World—with (00)7 top choices in most categories, plus nuggets worth passing along. In a whisper, of course.

BOND'S WORLD OF WOMEN

THE 007 BEST BOND GIRLS

1. **HONEY RYDER,** as played by Ursula Andress, in *Dr. No*. Her weapons of choice were that diving knife and a black widow spider, and her moment was rising from the sea like the goddess she was. Her backstory: Honey had lived all around the world while studying shells with her scientist father, whom she believed to have been killed by Dr. No. As for the spider: She once killed a man who raped her by putting a black widow spider in his mosquito net. "Did I do wrong?" she asks Bond, who, having just had a narrow escape from a tarantula in his own bed, replies: "Well, it wouldn't do to make a habit of it." A postscript on this theme of voracious animals: In the novel, Honey was, at one point, staked out on the beach by Dr. No to be eaten by land crabs. The scene was shot for the movie, but the crabs mostly just sat around Andress and barely crawled an inch.

2. **TATIANA ROMANOVA,** as played by Daniela Bianchi, in *From Russia with Love*.

3. **DOMINO DERVAL,** as played by Claudine Auger, in *Thunderball*.

4. **DOMINO PETACHI,** as played by Kim Basinger, in *Never Say Never Again*.

5. **TRACY/MRS. JAMES BOND,** as played Diana Rigg, in *On Her Majesty's Secret Service*.

6. **MELINA HAVELOCK,** as played by Carole Bouquet, in *For Your Eyes Only*.

7. **KISSY SUZUKI,** as played by Mie Hama, in *You Only Live Twice*.

BAD GIRLS

1. **ROSA KLEBB,** as played by Lotte Lenya, in *From Russia with Love* (whom you've read about already in these pages).

2. **PUSSY GALORE,** as played by Honor Blackman, in *Goldfinger*. The British actress, well known in her homeland as Dr. Gale in the TV series *The Avengers*, which would soon make a star of Diana Rigg, was, along with Rigg, one of two women who, as Bond Girls, were older than the Bond actor they played against (she was 38 when making *Goldfinger*). That's even if you count Deborah Kerr in the comic *Casino Royale*, because her Bond was David Niven, born in 1910.

3. **FIONA VOLPE,** as played by Luciana Paluzzi, in *Thunderball*.

4. **FATIMA BLUSH,** as played by Barbara Carrera, in *Never Say Never Again*.

5. **IRMA BUNT,** as played by Ilse Steppat, in *On Her Majesty's Secret Service*. Steppat's is an extraordinary story: Born in Germany in 1917, her role as Blofeld's assistant and henchwoman was her first appearance in an English-language film, and she made quite an impression. But she died of a heart attack at age 52, four days after the movie's release, and thus never was allowed to follow up on her newfound fame (and notoriety).

6. **MAY DAY,** as played by Grace Jones, in *A View to a Kill*—another woman you've learned about earlier in our book.

7. **ELEKTRA KING,** as played by Sophie Marceau, in *The World Is Not Enough*.

HONORABLE MENTION

WHO COULD BEAT a bench boasting Vesper Lynd, as played by Eva Green, in (Craig's) *Casino Royale*; Dink, as played by Margaret Nolan, in *Goldfinger*; Nurse Patricia, as played by Molly Peters, in *Thunderball*; Natalya Simonova, as played by Izabella Scorupco, in *GoldenEye*; Pam Bovier, as played by Carey Lowell, in *Licence to Kill*; and Jinx, as played by Halle Berry, in *Die Another Day*.

PAYING THE PRICE

1. **PAULA CAPLAN,** as played by Martine Beswick, in *Thunderball* wound up dead, and so did these other six.

2. **LISL,** as played by Cassandra Harris, in *For Your Eyes Only*. The real-life wife of Pierce Brosnan was visited by hubby on the set of her 1981 Roger Moore vehicle.

3. **JILL AND TILLY MASTERSON,** as played by Shirley Eaton and Tania Mallet, respectively, in *Goldfinger*.

4. **AKI,** as played by Akiko Wakabayashi, in *You Only Live Twice*.

5. **PLENTY O'TOOLE,** as played by Lana Wood, in *Diamonds Are Forever*. The younger sister of Natalie Wood, Lana was known for her role on the prime-time soap *Peyton Place*.

6. **MS. ANDERS,** as played by Maud Adams, in *The Man with the Golden Gun*.

7. **PARIS CARVER,** as played by Teri Hatcher, later of *Desperate Housewives*, in *Tomorrow Never Dies*.

POPPERFOTO/GETTY

SONY PICTURES/EVERETT

CORRECTING THE MI6 FILES

ALTHOUGH MANY CONSIDER Ursula Andress to be the first Bond Girl, that hallowed historical distinction in fact belongs to Eunice Gayson as Sylvia Trench, in both *Dr. No* and *From Russia with Love.* Early in the first film, before Andress makes her eye-opening entrance, Bond looks at his watch while kissing Trench to make sure he has enough time to finish what *she* has started. According to Gayson, director Terence Young's original plan was for her to play Trench in the first six films. But Young did not return to direct *Goldfinger*, and Gayson's character was dropped.

MI6 POP QUIZ

Which actress was voted the worst Bond Girl of all time by fans?

A) Tanya Roberts

B) Jill St. John

C) Lois Chiles

D) Denise Richards

Answer: D. Denise Richards, famous for lasting four years as Charlie Sheen's wife (2002–2006), was infamous with fans as Dr. Christmas Jones in 1999's *The World Is Not Enough.* Readers polled by the London *Daily Mail* felt that she set the Bond Girl back 20 years, an almost unnatural feat.

IN PRAISE OF BAD GUYS

BEST OF THE WORST

1. **ERNST STAVRO BLOFELD,** of course—as played by Anthony Dawson, Donald Pleasence, Telly Savalas and Charles Gray, plus Max von Sydow in the "unofficial" *Never Say Never Again.* In *From Russia with Love* and *Thunderball,* Blofeld is seen only from the neck down, impeccably dressed and petting a white cat. To keep the mystery of Blofeld's identity, he was listed in the closing credits of *Russia* as "Blofeld . . . ?" and was uncredited in *Thunderball.* In reality, it was actor Dawson in the fancy suit. Pleasence was the first to actually appear onscreen as a scar-faced, bald Blofeld, and it was his portrayal that was lampooned by Mike Myers as Dr. Evil in the hilarious *Austin Powers* spy comedies. Savalas was a more athletic Blofeld with no earlobes—a congenital trait of the de Bleuchamp family, of whom Blofeld insists he is the reigning Comte Balthazar de Bleuchamp in *On Her Majesty's Secret Service.*

2. **DR. NO,** as played by Joseph Wiseman.

3. **AURIC GOLDFINGER,** as played by Gert Fröbe, in *Goldfinger.*

4. **EMILIO LARGO,** as played by Adolfo Celi, in *Thunderball.*

5. **FRANCISCO SCARAMANGA,** as played by Christopher Lee, in *The Man with the Golden Gun.*

6. **FRANZ SANCHEZ,** as played by Robert Davi, in *Licence to Kill.*

7. **LE CHIFFRE,** as played by Mads Mikkelsen, in the 2006 *Casino Royale.*

EVERETT

HORRIBLE HENCHMEN

1. **PROFESSOR DENT** in *Dr. No.* Anthony Dawson, anonymous as the physical presence of Blofeld in the second and fourth Bond films, played Dent in *Dr. No.*

2. **DONALD "RED" GRANT,** the paranoid homicidal hitman played by Robert Shaw in *From Russia with Love.*

3. **ODDJOB,** above, as played by Harold Sakata, in *Goldfinger.* Opposite: Sakata moonlights during the *Goldfinger* shoot in his other job, pro wrestling (he's in the foreground, his lethal steel-brimmed bowler resting on the corner post).

4. **MR. VARGAS,** harpooned by Bond in *Thunderball,* as played by Philip Locke.

5. **MR. WINT AND MR. KIDD,** as played by Bruce Glover and Putter Smith, in *Diamonds Are Forever.*

6. **NICK NACK,** as played by *Fantasy Island* fixture Hervé Villechaize, in *The Man with the Golden Gun.*

7. **JAWS,** as played by Richard Kiel, in *The Spy Who Loved Me* and *Moonraker.*

007 NEAR-DEATH EXPERIENCES

1. **THE TARANTULA SCENE** in *Dr. No.* According to the film's production designer, Ken Adam, Sean Connery was reluctant to perform with a tarantula climbing over him. He was right to be, for as director Terence Young later recalled, "We had to put glass on Sean for obvious reasons, because this was a lethal animal and it had its poison sac. And he could have in fact been killed by it. We had a doctor on the set." Stunt coordinator Bob Simmons drew the unlucky assignment of interacting with the poisonous arachnid for close-ups that would be edited into the Connery sequence, and later called it his most frightening stunt ever.

2. **BOND'S DANCE OF DEATH** with Rosa Klebb and her poison-tipped shoe blade in *From Russia with Love,* a scene that occurred not too very long after Red Grant's attempted execution of 007—another close call for our hero.

3. *GOLDFINGER'S* **LASER RAY;** enough said.

4. **THE MOTORIZED TRACTION TABLE** and the shark pool in *Thunderball.*

5. **THE COFFIN CREMATION** in *Diamonds Are Forever.*

6. **THE ESCAPE** from alligators in *Live and Let Die.*

7. **BOND'S TORTURE** by Le Chiffre in *Casino Royale.* This scene has renderings from the extraordinarily mild in the 1954 TV depiction to the elongated and truly terrible in the Fleming novel and its faithful depiction in the 2006 film.

ENEMY LINES

1. **BLOFELD:** "Siamese fighting fish, fascinating creatures, brave but on the whole stupid. Yes, they're stupid. Except for the occasional one such as we have here—who lets the other two fight while he waits—waits until the survivor is so exhausted he cannot defend himself. And then like SPECTRE, he strikes."
—*From Russia with Love*

2. **BOND:** "Red wine with fish. Well, that should have told me something."
   RED GRANT: "You may know the right wines, but you're the one on his knees."
—*From Russia with Love*

3. **BOND:** "Do you expect me to talk?"
   GOLDFINGER (about to cut Bond in half with a laser): "No, Mr. Bond. I expect you to die!"
—*Goldfinger*

4. **FIONA VOLPE:** "Oh, I forgot your ego, Mr. Bond. James Bond, who only has to make love to a woman and she hears every choir singing. She immediately repents and returns to the side of right and virtue. But not this one! What a blow it must have been, you having a failure."
   BOND: "Well, you can't win them all."
—*Thunderball*

5. **MR. WINT:** "The scorpion."
   MR. KIDD: "One of nature's finest killers, Mr. Wint."
   MR. WINT: "One is never too old to learn from a master, Mr. Kidd."
—*Diamonds Are Forever*

6. **FRANZ SANCHEZ:** "What did he promise you—his heart? Give her his heart!"
—*Licence to Kill*

7. **BOND:** "You're really quite insane."
   ELLIOT CARVER: "The distance between insanity and genius is measured only by success."
—*Tomorrow Never Dies*

HONORABLE MENTION

ALEC TREVELYAN, an MI6 turncoat in *GoldenEye:* "I might as well ask if all those vodka martinis silenced the screams of all the men you've killed. Or if you've found forgiveness in the arms of all those willing women for the dead ones you failed to protect."

LOOMIS DEAN

MI6 POP QUIZ

In which movie did Bond describe his dispatching of a villain thusly: "He met his Waterloo"?

A) *On Her Majesty's Secret Service*

B) *Live and Let Die*

C) *The Living Daylights*

D) *Die Another Day*

Answer: C. In *The Living Daylights,* after Timothy Dalton as Bond crushes arms dealer Brad Whitaker to death with a solid marble bust of the Duke of Wellington, the British general who defeated Napoleon at Waterloo.

STUFF

BMT 216 A

WHEELS

1. **THE SUNBEAM ALPINE SERIES II ROADSTER CONVERTIBLE,** rented and driven by Bond in *Dr. No,* most notably in a scene where our hero drives under a truck to escape from pursuing hit men.

The car was reportedly borrowed from a local resident during filming in Jamaica.

2. **BOND'S VINTAGE BENTLEY.** This car first appeared as a personal passion project in the first novel, and Bentleys began their run as Bond cars of choice in

the second movie, *From Russia with Love.*

3. **THE ASTON MARTIN DB5,** such an icon in its Q-souped *Goldfinger* version (above). Bond filmmakers through the years have felt compelled to bring back Aston Martins—the V8, the Vanquish, etc.

4. **THE LOTUS ESPRIT SUBMARINE CAR,** one of three Lotuses to appear in the series and one of the many reasons *The Spy Who Loved Me* was such a thrilling thriller.

5. **FOUR BMWs,** including the last one, which was sliced in half by a helicopter in *The World Is Not Enough.* But the cars were upstaged by the BMW R1200 motorcycle that Bond stole and piloted during an escape in *Tomorrow Never Dies.*

6. **AKI'S 1966 TOYOTA 2000 GT,** with which she saves Bond's life twice in *You Only Live Twice.* For the film, Toyota Motor Corporation created a special convertible version of its superfast sports car, one equipped with an audio/video communications center behind the driver's and passenger's seats on the back wall of the leather interior.

7. **BOND'S ROLLS-ROYCE SILVER SHADOW** in *Licence to Kill*—because of course we have to include a Rolls-Royce.

VILLAINOUS VEHICLES

1. **THE HEARSE** full of hit men in *Dr. No.*

2. **GOLDFINGER'S** solid gold Rolls-Royce Phantom 337.

3. **THE FLAME-THROWING** marsh buggy from *Dr. No.*

4. **THE ROCKET-FIRING** BSA Lightning motorcycle from *Thunderball.*

5. **THE ROCKET-FIRING** pimpmobile in *Live and Let Die.*

6. **SCARAMANGA'S FLYING CAR** in *The Man with the Golden Gun.*

7. **ZAO'S WEAPONS-PACKED** Jaguar from *Die Another Day.*

FLYING, DIVING

1. **AS YOU KNOW** from earlier in our book, Bond donned a jet pack, which is among his coolest-ever flight gimmicks, in *Thunderball,* then the pack was featured in a short cameo in *Die Another Day.*

2. **THE LITTLE NELLIE** autogyro—the solo-pilot copter in *You Only Live Twice*—was shipped by Q in four suitcases, then assembled on a Japanese island.

3. **THE ACROSTAR MINI JET** of *Octopussy* helps Bond fly under the radar of a country that closely resembles Cuba.

4. **THE JACKKNIFE GLIDERS** of *Die Another Day* were shaped like fighter planes.

5. **THE UNDERWATER PROPULSION UNIT** in *Thunderball* shot Bond into battle and, once he was there, supplied him with spear guns, explosive bottles and a searchlight.

6. **SIMILARLY LOADED** with weaponry, the *Moonraker* speedboat featured heat-seeking torpedoes, mines and a hang-glider escape option.

7. **THE MINI Q-BOAT** in *The World Is Not Enough* upped the ante, with *dual* heat-seeking torpedoes and the ability to dive.

BEST BAD GUY GADGETS EVER

1. **ROSA KLEBB'S** shoe with the hidden blade (above) in *From Russia with Love.*

2. **DONALD GRANT'S** wristwatch with the concealed strangling wire, also in *From Russia with Love.*

3. **DR. NO'S** hydraulic metal hands.

4. **ODDJOB'S** razor-sharp steel-brimmed bowler in *Goldfinger.*

5. **TEE HEE'S** mechanical arm from *Live and Let Die.*

6. **SCARAMANGA'S** golden gun in . . . (well, you know).

7. **THE BUZZ SAW YO-YO** in *Octopussy.*

Q BRANCH DECLASSIFIED

1. **THE WALTHER PPK HANDGUN.** Geoffrey Boothroyd, a gun enthusiast, found a flaw in *Casino Royale.* "Certain inaccuracies in the book made me write to Fleming and say that I didn't think that Bond was going to last very long if he used a two-fire Beretta pistol, which is a ladies' gun and not a very nice lady at that," Boothroyd later recalled. With Boothroyd's approval, Fleming rearmed 007 with a Walther PPK 7.25 in the sixth novel, *Dr. No.* He also introduced then, in tribute, the character of MI6 weapons quartermaster Major Boothroyd, a.k.a. Q. In *Skyfall,* the Walther is a personalized PPK/S with a palm-print reader.

2. **THE ATTACHÉ CASE,** issued by Q and deployed to great effect in *From Russia with Love.* Just about everything was useful: the 40 rounds of ammo, the flat throwing knife, the folding sniper's rifle, the 50 gold sovereigns and, of course, the exploding tear-gas cartridge.

3. **THE HOMING DEVICES,** large and small, issued in *Goldfinger:* Stick them to a car or insert them into a shoe, then follow along.

4. **THE REBREATHERS,** whether in *Thunderball* or *Die Another Day,* where an underwater Bond gets bonus oxygen.

5. **ALL THOSE WRISTWATCHES,** more than Swatch: the Geiger Counter, the Buzz Saw Watch with Hyper-intensified Magnetic Field Projection, the Laser Watch . . . Ian Fleming said Bond's wrist bore a Rolex, and Cubby Broccoli loaned his own Rolex Submariner to Sean Connery for *Dr. No.* The Submariner was Bond's watch until 1977, when he switched to a Seiko. After five films he returned to the Submariner in 1987, but from *GoldenEye* forward he has sported an Omega Seamaster.

6. **THE PHILIPS GAS-SPOUTING KEY RING,** which additionally has keys that can pick 90 percent of the world's locks.

7. **THE ERICSSON REMOTE-CONTROL CELL PHONE,** which—really!—was way cool back in the day.

BOND AT WORK AND PLAY

REPARTEE: THE WIT OF BOND

1. **"BOND . . . JAMES BOND"**—one of the most legendary introductions in cinematic history; it has been compared to Humphrey Bogart's bow in *Casablanca* (although *Dr. No* director Terence Young intended it as a takeoff on Paul Muni's introduction in the 1939 film *Juarez*). As with many great things, the scene's creation wasn't as easy as it might appear. Bond had to light his cigarette while saying the line, but the timing was proving difficult to coordinate. Finally, Young had Connery simply say, "Bond," light his cigarette, pause a beat to snap his lighter shut, then finish with "James Bond." The rhythm proved perfect.

2. **"SHE'S HAD HER KICKS"**—spoken by Connery's Bond in *From Russia with Love* after his dance of death with Rosa Klebb and her poison-tip shoe, a dance that ends when Bond Girl Tatiana Romanova shoots Klebb dead.

3. **"SHOCKING! POSITIVELY SHOCKING"**— Connery's Bond again, in *Goldfinger,* after he has electrocuted his would-be assassin by tossing an electric heater into a bathtub full of water that the thug had fallen into during the fight.

4. **"I THINK HE GOT THE POINT"**— Connery yet again in *Thunderball,* after killing SPECTRE agent Vargas with a spear gun, pinning him to a palm tree. This film marked the brief reunion of Connery and director Young, who, together in the first two films, developed this manner of repartee and egregious punning that they felt was necessary to allow viewers

MGM/EVERETT

to warm to their sex-and-violence subject matter and a hero who, as the early ads had it, kills "whom he pleases, where he pleases, when he pleases." Young later recalled his strategy in a way that would do Bond proud: "I said, 'Sean, for Christ's sake, we've got to make this picture a little bit amusing. It's the only way we're going to get away with murder.'"

5. **"DO YOU MIND IF MY FRIEND** sits this one out? She's just dead"—also Connery, also *Thunderball,* after SPECTRE assassin Fiona Volpe dies in his arms on the dance floor, having taken a bullet meant for him. Bond sits her body down next to some tourists for a very long rest. Young continued, in reminiscing about the dialogue: "Sean and I made an awful lot of those gags up on the set." The first time they went for a laugh was in *Dr. No* when Bond drove a dead enemy agent to Government House and told the officer on duty, "Make sure he doesn't get away." Audiences giggled, and Young and Connery knew they were on to something.

6. **"SHE ALWAYS DID ENJOY** a good squeeze"—spoken by Pierce Brosnan as Bond in *GoldenEye* after disposing of the deadly Xenia Onatopp (who had enjoyed executing men in bed with her "killer thighs") by throwing a zip line into the blades of her helicopter, which caused her to be hoisted into the air and crushed to death against a tree.

7. **"SORRY. THAT LAST HAND** [small pause] nearly killed me"—uttered by Daniel Craig as Bond in the 2006 *Casino Royale* after he had been poisoned, had clinically died and had been resuscitated between poker hands. The line and its delivery mark a small triumph of drollery for the "more serious" Craig, who went a long additional way in proving his deft comedic timing and amiable sense of humor when he (in character as Bond) went to Buckingham Palace to escort Queen Elizabeth II to the 2012 Olympic Opening Ceremonies for a parachute entrance into the stadium.

HONORABLE MENTION

"THIS NEVER HAPPENED to the other fella," declared George Lazenby's 007 after having a woman leave him hanging in *On Her Majesty's Secret Service.* This shows how far Bond could go to elicit a laugh. Roger Moore always went furthest, and once explained, "I think Sean, trying to analyze it, once said that his jokes came from left field, and I let people know that a joke was coming. And I suppose that's true. I said [to audiences], 'Hey. I'm having a lot of fun doing this and I hope you are enjoying watching it.'"

DANJAQ/EON/UA/KOBAL/ART RESOURCE, NY

THOSE WACKY STUNTS

1. **BOND TORCHING** a fleet of SPECTRE boats in *From Russia with Love.*

2. **THE TWO-WHEEL** tilted-car escape in *Diamonds Are Forever* (above).

3. **THE ONE-LEGGED** skiing in *On Her Majesty's Secret Service.*

4. **THE SKIING PARACHUTE JUMP** in *The Spy Who Loved Me* (even cooler than the parachuting-with-the-queen jump to open the Olympics).

5. **THE FIGHT** in free fall from *Moonraker.*

6. **THE TANKER TRUCK CHASE** sequence in *Licence to Kill,* with Bond making his truck pop a wheelie (also that memorable waterskiing-without-skis bit earlier on).

7. **THE BUNGEE JUMP** off the dam in *GoldenEye.* Just by the way, when the publicists insist, "He did all his own stunts," take the grain of salt . . . Sean Connery performed in a more innocent age, and did more than most—certainly more than Moore. Connery once broke his wrist, and had his back hurt by Oddjob in *Goldfinger.*

WINDING DOWN AT THE BAR

BOND AND HIS MAKER, Ian Fleming, were both famous booze-hounds. In the second novel, *Live and Let Die,* the spy goes on the wagon to get fit for his perilous swim across the bay to the Big Man's evil island, then figures he should have a stiffish shooter before entering the water. In the books and even more so the movies, where some options have the smell of product placement, Bond's many cocktail choices have included the famous vodka martini (opposite, being quaffed by Pierce Brosnan)—which, yes, he prefers shaken, not stirred—then also, depending upon mood and locale, bourbon and branch water, a mojito, even a mint julep.

FRIENDS AND FAMILY

MI6 POP QUIZ

In what Bond opus did 007 actually refuse the affections of a Bond Girl?

A) *Live and Let Die*

B) *The Man with the Golden Gun*

C) *For Your Eyes Only*

D) *On Her Majesty's Secret Service*

Answer: C: When the barely legal Bibi Dahl is found waiting in bed for Bond, 007 draws the line and says, "I don't think your Uncle Ari would approve." Bibi exclaims: "Him? He thinks I'm still a virgin." To which Bond replies, "Yes, well, you get your clothes on—and I'll buy you an ice cream." Roger Moore was in his mid-50s in 1981 and would have caused Bond to look like a lecherous old man had he played the scene per Bibi's designs. We were spared that image, and today Bond is young, handsome and virile again, thanks to Daniel Craig. Ever thus, may it ever be thus. Another 50 years, please.

BOND IN LOVE

1. **ALONE AT LAST?** Not quite. In *Dr. No*, Bond and Honey escape from the evil one's exploding headquarters in a rowboat, and there Bond figures the heavy lifting is over and starts kissing Honey passionately. But here comes Felix Leiter and his U.S. Marines' rescue effort, and Bond has to take evasive measures once more.

2. **STAYING UNDERCOVER.** After Bond and Pussy Galore escape a crashing Learjet via parachute in *Goldfinger,* Pussy tries to signal Leiter's helicopter. But Bond insists, "This is no time to be rescued!" and pulls the parachute fabric over them as the credits roll.

3. **TELLTALE BUBBLES.** In *Thunderball,* Bond and Domino, in scuba gear, swim toward each other offshore in Nassau. They embrace, and slowly sink behind a small reef, from which emerges an enormous rush of bubbles. What the heck's going on in there? "I hope we didn't frighten the fish," says Bond afterwards.

4. **SUBOPTIMAL.** "They'll never find us," Bond assures Kissy in *You Only Live Twice* as the two make love in a solitary life raft in the middle of the ocean. Suddenly, M's submarine surfaces beneath them, lifting the raft out of the water to rest on the deck. "Tell him to come below and report," says M. "It'll be a pleasure, sir," says Moneypenny as the movie ends.

5. **ASTRONAUGHTY.** Bond joins the 375-mile-high club when he makes love to Holly Goodhead in zero gravity aboard an orbiting space shuttle in *Moonraker.* "I think he's attempting reentry, sir," says Q, monitoring Bond's "progress" from Earth.

6. **A FRIEND IN NEED.** Though she had been elusive, Chinese agent Wai Lin finally falls for 007 when, while she's chained underwater and drowning, Bond offers the kiss of life by sharing his oxygen in *Tomorrow Never Dies.*

7. **THE WOMAN HE WED.** On the run from SPECTRE in the Swiss Alps in *On Her Majesty's Secret Service,* Bond and Tracy drive into a warm barn where, as a blizzard rages outside, Bond proposes marriage. The lady says yes, and . . . (below).

THE GANG DOWN AT MI6

1. **WE START WITH M.** Everything trickles down from the top—attitude, confidence, mission—and the chief executive at Bond's place of work (as much a home as Bond has ever had) has always been M. The role was played by Bernard Lee from *Dr. No* through *Moonraker,* John Huston in the spoof version of *Casino Royale,* Edward Fox in *Never Say Never Again,* Robert Brown from *Octopussy* through *Licence to Kill* and has belonged to Judi Dench since *GoldenEye* and continues to be through *Skyfall:* a distinguished roster indeed.

2. **MISS MONEYPENNY,** as played by Lois Maxwell (opposite), Caroline Bliss and Samantha Bond (with Maxwell on the opening pages of this chapter) throughout the franchise. Maxwell was nearly Bond's first conquest, Sylvia Trench; *Dr. No*'s director, Terence Young, had offered Maxwell a choice of two roles, and she couldn't imagine herself playing golf in Bond's bedroom wearing only his pajama top. She opted for Moneypenny, M's secretary, with the stipulation that she be allowed to create a backstory for the character and not be made to wear her hair in a bun with a pencil over her ear. As Maxwell later explained it, "When [Bond] was

a tea boy and [Moneypenny] was in the secretarial pool, they had gone off together for a lovely bank holiday weekend to a rose covered cottage and had 'fully appreciated each other's qualities.' But she realized that if she allowed herself to fall in love with him, he would probably break her heart. And he knew that if he allowed himself to fall in love with her, then he'd never get his 00. That was the background of their [relationship] in the office."

3. **MAJOR BOOTHROYD—**better known as Q—as played by Peter Burton and Desmond Llewelyn. John Cleese began as Llewelyn's assistant and then briefly became the gadgetmeister in *Die Another Day* after Llewelyn's death. The latest Q is played by Ben Whishaw in *Skyfall.*

4. **FELIX LEITER.** Okay, not properly MI6—not even British—but this CIA operative is greatly respected by Bond: as much a colleague as any. When the filmmakers behind the TV *Casino Royale* in 1954 Americanized the Bond character, "Clarence" Leiter became Bond's British contact.

5. **BILL TANNER,** M's chief of staff, Bond's biggest defender in the agency and his sometime golf partner after hours, perhaps most memorably incarnated by the wonderful Michael Kitchen (*Foyle's War*) in the 1990s.

6. **CHARLES ROBINSON.** This gets a little confusing: He is also an MI6 chief of staff, and in fact appeared together with Bill Tanner in *The World Is Not Enough.* As played by the black actor Colin Salmon, he represented, in a three-movie tenure, MI6's efforts at diversity.

7. **JACK WADE.** The bluff CIA contact, a kind of surrogate Leiter, gets over his initial impression of Bond as a "stiff-ass Brit" and is quickly calling Bond "Jimbo," a nickname to which James is unaccustomed. Ian Fleming and James Bond much liked and admired Americans. The feeling was always mutual.

JUST ONE MORE

WHEN MILITARY INTELLIGENCE operatives or foreign correspondents needed to know all about the world during wartimes hot or cold, LIFE was part of their required weekly reading. Little did Ian Fleming know, in 1948, that 18 years later he would be on the cover—for having invented a spy.

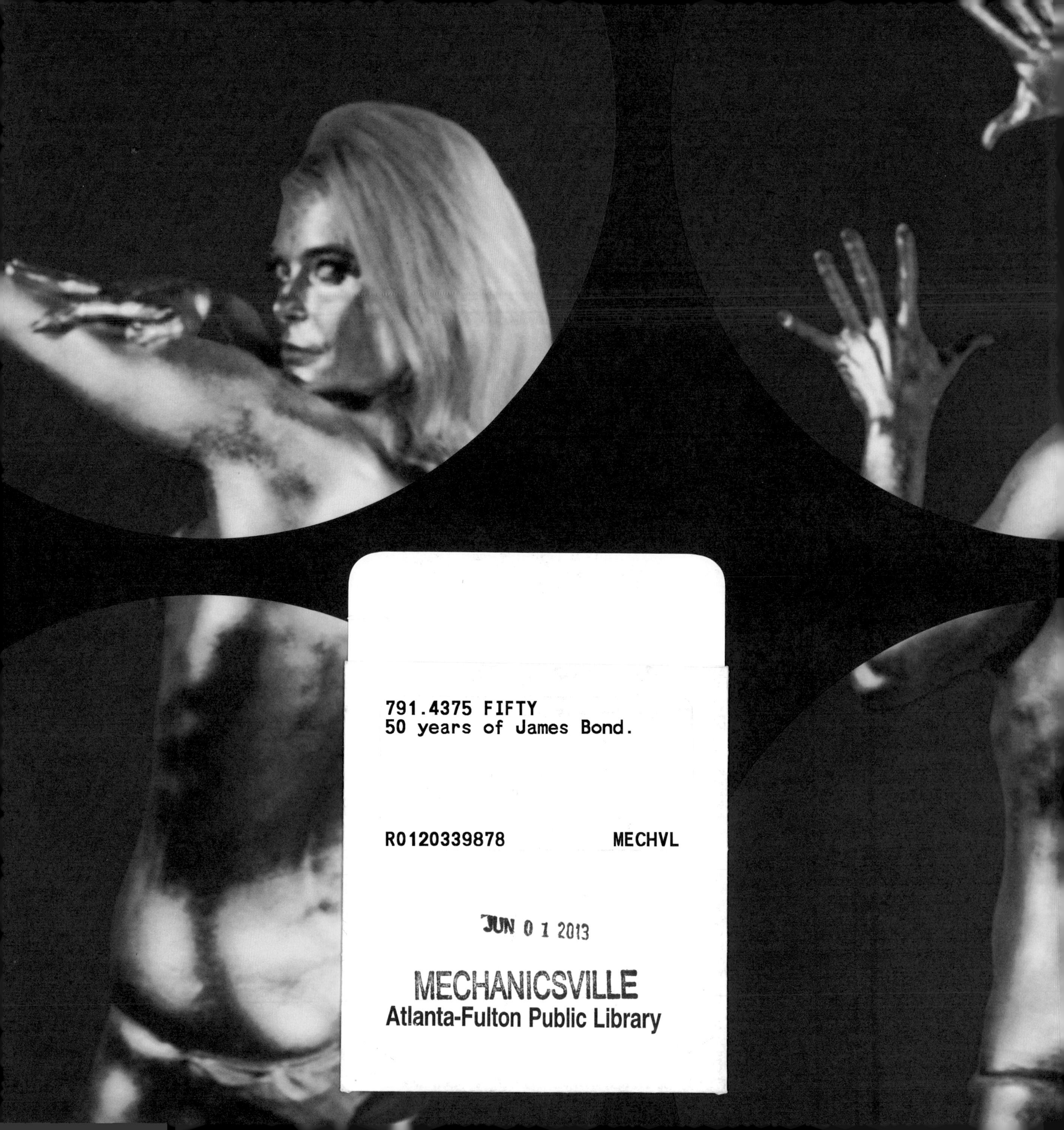